D1595652

1. Jerry Berry, 3rd row center

2. Tony Gibson, 3rd row left

3. John Griffin, front left

4. Lionel Grimes, (not pictured)

5. Mel Hamilton, last row left

6. Ron Hill, (not pictured)

7. Willie Hysaw, front right

8. Jim Isaac, last row right

9. Earl Lee, front center

10. Tony McGee, (not pictured)

11. Don Meadows, 2nd row left behind John

12. Ivie Moore, behind Earl center

13. Joe Williams, 3rd row right

14. Ted Williams, (not pictured)

Black 14

The Rise, Fall and Rebirth of Wyoming Football

by

Ryan Thorburn

Burning Daylight

Published by Burning Daylight, an imprint of
Pearn and Associates, Inc., Boulder, Colorado.
For information about our products and services
please contact us at happypoet@hotmail.com,
(720) 620-4499.

Cover design by Anne Kilgore.
Front photo by Art Shay, Sports Illustrated, Nov. 3, 1969.
Photographs in the last section are provided as a courtesy of
the University of Wyoming Photo Service.

Acknowledgments

This book would not have been possible without the help of
the Sports Information Department at the University of
Wyoming, especially Tim Harkins. A special thank you to Phil
White, whose advice, direction, research and editing
suggestions were of great help during the writing process.
Also, thank you to everyone involved in the Black 14 incident
and Wyoming football who shared their memories and stories
during interviews.

Library of Congress Control Number: 2009928221

Thorburn, Ryan 1971
Black 14, by Ryan Thorburn. First Edition.
ISBN 978-0-9777318-9-3 paper.

For my girls—

Nicole, Madelyn, Gabrielle and Peyton

Contents

Preface

When I think about Wyoming football, I think about my grandfather, Ray Thorburn, a faithful Cowboys fan who was born in Wyarno, Wyoming, on July 23, 1918. Ray was buried in Buffalo, Wyoming, on July 23, 2007, my 36th birthday. I had an unbreakable bond with him, and it was natural that his enthusiasm for Cowboy football would rub off on me.

Like most World War II veterans, Ray kept the unpleasant memories of sacrifice and service between himself and his peers from the greatest generation. As a future reporter, however, I did manage to coax a few stories out of him.

Ray arrived in Hawaii weeks after the Japanese attack on Pearl Harbor on December 7, 1941, but the fatally wounded battleships were still billowing smoke. After spending Christmas in a foxhole and then participating in the Battle of Midway from June 4-7, 1942, he was transferred back to Honolulu and worked at a hospital. He was once given a rare afternoon off—the day Franklin Delano Roosevelt decided to schedule a visit. Ray's superior told him he could still take the personal time if he wished, but that would mean missing out on a chance to meet the president.

Since Ray had a tennis date with a fetching young female . . . well, surely the Commander in Chief would understand.

My grandfather was a brilliant poker player and brought home enough winnings from the war to open up his own small business. Ray also invested in season tickets and painfully long car rides from Buffalo down to Laramie, Wyoming, to support Wyoming football as the program was entering its golden era.

The real beauty of the Wyoming football tradition is that the Cowboys are a subject that tough old guys are willing to talk about with their sons and grandsons and even their great-granddaughters.

My love affair with the Pokes officially began on October 24, 1981. I was 10 years old but can still remember the details of that fall Saturday better than almost any sporting event I've ever attended. And I've covered close to 200 NFL games, the Stanley Cup finals and the World Series during my newspaper career.

Ray picked me up in Casper that crisp morning and we drove down to Laramie in his stylish, mint green Mercury Marquis for the Wyoming-Brigham Young game. His day started two hours north in Buffalo and we had to navigate blizzard conditions en route to War Memorial Stadium, more than a two-hour drive to the south of my childhood home on a good day.

Just like many diehard Cowboys faithful, Ray and my grandma Madelyn were willing to travel great distances and on dangerous roads to support the football program that they adored. It's not easy being a Wyoming fan. The rides home after bitter defeats felt like they were being driven on the road to perdition.

On days like this one, however, all of the painful losses and disappointments were forgotten.

The Cowboys were supposed to be the latest victim of Heisman Trophy candidate Jim McMahon and the 13th-ranked Cougars. Right on cue, BYU roared out to a 14-0 lead before we had finished our first round of hot chocolate. Then the snow really started falling, and Ray tried to talk me into hitting the highway early and listening on the car radio to the rest of what would surely be a punch-to-the-gut loss.

No chance. We're staying. Can I have another hot chocolate?

Wyoming rewarded my loyalty by rattling off 33 unanswered points and piling up 474 yards of total offense as quarterback Phil Davis outplayed McMahon. The final score was Wyoming 33, BYU 20. The Cowboys clobbered Colorado State 55-21 on the same field a week later and finished the season with an 8-3 record.

Since that day, my heroes have always been Cowboys.

But for fans like Ray and my dad, these weren't the best of times. During my father's Laramie days as a University of Wyoming student in the late '60s, the Pokes never lost a home game. They beat Florida State in the Sun Bowl and played in the Sugar Bowl. The roster was loaded with future NFL players like Jim Kiick, Vic Washington, Mike Dirks, Larry Nels and Jerry DePoyster. And the list goes on.

Those were the true glory days. So what happened to the program? The Black 14, my dad would say without elaboration.

The 1969 season brought the end of a dominant era and remained a sore subject no one in Wyoming seemed to want to talk about when I was growing up. It's a story I've always been fascinated with.

While researching this project I had a chance to talk to a lot of great people associated with the program in the 1960s, some famous and some infamous, some loved and some who felt loathed. I'd like to thank everyone who was willing to share their stories and hope you enjoy a book that covers some of the good, bad and ugly times that make Wyoming football so unforgettable.

—Ryan Thorburn

The 'Pokes Go Marching In

No one crashes a party like the Cowboys. Decades before the Bowl Championship Series existed and 41 years before the University of Utah's stunning victory over Alabama at the Superdome, it was the Wyoming football program—ranked in the top five nationally and riding a 14-game win streak—that found itself in the national spotlight at the Sugar Bowl.

When Lloyd Eaton's 'Pokes accepted the invitation to participate in the prestigious game after finishing the 1967 season with a 10-0 record, one fan described the bowl bid as "the biggest thing since statehood." (1)

December 31, 1967, was a quiet night back on campus in Laramie and across the state of Wyoming—which had a population of only 330,000 at the time—because the big New Year's Eve party had been moved to New Orleans. At least 10,000 fans made the trip to the Sugar Bowl to watch Wyoming face Louisiana State University.

For one week, Bourbon Street was brown and gold—Mardi Gras with cowboy hats.

"Wyoming people loved football and loved to party. And they showed New Orleans," recalled Keith

Burman, a Cowboys' season ticket holder since 1959 who made the trip from the Gem City to the Big Easy. "Bourbon Street was something else. Wyoming people had never seen anything like that. They were amazed but they jumped right in . . . .

"There were a lot of cowboy hats, a lot of cowboy boots. You didn't have trouble finding Wyoming people that night."

Wyoming fans claim that bartenders at historic hotels such as the Place d'Armes, the Price Conti and the Monte Leone were running low on whiskey as kickoff neared.

"The Cowboys took over the French Quarter," said Dave Montgomery, who was a member of the UW marching band that performed at halftime. "A lot of it had to do with the fact that we were playing the home team. If we were playing Ohio State or Notre Dame, there would have been a lot of their supporters out. But it was all Wyoming fans and it was a big party . . . .

"I think after three 'Hurricanes' on Bourbon Street I tried to propose to a parking meter."

Meanwhile, at the Fontainebleau Hotel, it was all business for Eaton and the team. Despite the large contingent of Cowboys' fans, this was a road game for

Wyoming, which had a lot to prove against favored Southeastern Conference (SEC) power LSU.

"If we went to Bourbon Street it was a brief visit," says graceful UW wide receiver Gene Huey, a junior on the Sugar Bowl team. "The coaches definitely had curfews and bed checks for the players."

Other than adhering to Eaton's strict code of discipline, the Cowboys were treated like rock stars by their adoring fan base.

"For a 13-year-old from Laramie, to be in the Fontainebleau Hotel on New Year's Eve was pretty cool," said Sally Ann Shurmur, the daughter of Fritz Shurmur, the defensive coach on the '67 team who would become Wyoming's next head coach in 1971. "My favorite thing was taking the elevator down to the lobby and just watching all the players and fans who were dressed up. I sat there for hours with my beloved Nana and we just watched all of the people."

All eyes were on Wyoming football.

Gene Huey grew up in Uniontown, Pennsylvania, where men of all colors earned a living and respect working side by side in coal mines and steel mills. Football under the Friday night lights was a great distraction for people and gave a few of the town's gridiron legends a chance to step into the national spotlight.

As a young man, Huey had a great role model to look up to in Ernie Davis, the Syracuse star who became the first African-American to win the Heisman Trophy in 1961. Davis lived in Uniontown until moving with his mother and stepfather to Emira, New York, at the age of 12.

Sandy Stephens, the first black quarterback at the University of Minnesota, developed his skills in the impressive junior and senior high programs of Uniontown before leading the Gophers to a national championship (1960) and the program's only Rose Bowl appearances (1960 and 1961).

Former Indianapolis and Super Bowl winning head coach Tony Dungy told Huey, who has been an assistant coach with the NFL's Colts since 1992, that Stephens is the reason he went to Minnesota as a player.

"Uniontown was a great place to grow up. It was a very diverse community," Huey said. "My own recollection of my childhood is that it was pretty good. You don't see certain things until you get older and visit different places."

One of the assistant coaches on the Uniontown High School team, Fred Answine, had played baseball at Wyoming. He sent some game film featuring Huey to one of Eaton's bright young assistants with an eye for talent—Paul Roach.

"I asked Paul about coming out for a visit," said Huey, whose other scholarship offers were from small colleges. SEC schools didn't recruit blacks at that time. "He said, 'Oh, sure.' But he knew he had me and the visit never materialized."

Huey had always wanted to travel and meet people from different parts of the country. He was also a big fan of westerns, including the hit television series "Laramie," and decided to take a chance on Wyoming.

So the wide-eyed young man bought a one-way train ticket for $55 in Connersville, Pennsylvania, and headed west. Upon his arrival in Laramie, Huey quickly realized that he had joined a special group of players from around the country that included Vic Washington, Jim Kiick and Larry Nels.

In 1966, the Cowboys finished 10-1, including a 28-20 victory over Florida State in the Sun Bowl. In 1968, UW won a share of its third consecutive Western Athletic Conference (WAC) championship. These were indeed the best of times for Wyoming football.

"It was a great time in Wyoming football because you had great players and great teams," Montgomery said. "We were winning championships, beating teams like Arizona State and crushing BYU and Colorado State. Every Saturday was a huge event, it was just huge. War Memorial Stadium was packed, kids were lined up ahead of time to get in. There were some other great times with Paul Roach and the Holiday Bowls in the late 80s, but nothing like that run in the 60s."

The 34th annual Sugar Bowl was played on Monday, January 1, 1968, at Tulane Stadium. A crowd of 72,858 turned out to see the Tigers take on the upstarts from the WAC.

"The Pokes were really outnumbered in the crowd," Roach, the iconic Wyoming athletic director and head coach who was an innovative offensive assistant on Eaton's staff during that era, recalled. "It was pretty noisy and a little tough for us to hear at times, especially in some of the critical situations. But we handled that pretty well."

Wyoming played like a team that belonged in the Sugar Bowl and the national spotlight, silencing the home crowd and perhaps stunning the national television audience by taking a 13-0 lead into the halftime locker room. Kiick scored on a 1-yard run, and Jerry DePoyster added the extra points and field goals of 24 and 49 yards for the Cowboys.

"We were very worried by the half," Tigers center Barry Wilson told reporters after the game.

The rain, which had been pouring all week, turned into a drizzle as the UW band took to the soggy field to perform at the intermission.

"I remember we had crappy band uniforms. They were horrible, just old and in bits and pieces," Montgomery said. "So in the time between when we got the bid and left for New Orleans, all of the members of the band went in and got fitted for brown slacks, gold blazers and nice Stetson cowboy hats. The band got a completely new look because we were going to play on national television at halftime . . . . I called my mom and asked how long we were on television and she said, 'About two minutes.'"

LSU had only mustered one first down and 38 yards against Shurmur's salty defensive unit, which entered the game ranked No. 1 nationally against the run (42.3 yards allowed per game) and No. 1 in total defense (185.2 yards per game).

Alan Simpson was in the stands watching the game with his wife Ann. The young attorney who would become a U.S. Senator representing Wyoming from 1979-97, played nose guard for the Cowboys in the early 50s, and usually keeps a close eye on the defensive line play through his binoculars when attending games.

Throughout the first half Simpson saw Larry Nels, the Cowboys' immovable defensive tackle, controlling the line of scrimmage. But Nels spent the second half watching the action from the sideline with a broken ankle.

"When Larry Nels went down, I said to Ann, 'Watch out, they're going to go right up that hole,'" Simpson said. "And some third-string tailback made about 120 yards."

Sure enough, the LSU coaching staff turned to a fresh third-string tailback named Glenn Smith, a New Orleans high school legend, to save the day. The sophomore started moving the chains and scored on a 1-yard run to cut the deficit to 13-7 after the third quarter.

The deeper Tigers had used the break to regroup and were starting to wear down Wyoming's defense with a more determined rushing attack, and the hometown crowd came alive.

"It's a game we felt like we should have won. It was played in their territory. The old Tulane Stadium seated 75,000 to 80,000, and it seemed very quiet until they started scoring," Gordon Cramer, a senior offensive lineman on the '67 team, said decades later. "It was like having the TV on with the sound off until they finally had something to cheer about." (2)

Tommy Morel completed the comeback with a pair of touchdown receptions thrown by quarterback Nelson Stokley. A missed extra point kept Wyoming within seven points and set up some last-second drama.

"LSU used 44 players, two units on offense and defense, and they substituted freely," Roach said. "Wyoming, maybe during the game we used 26 to 28 players it seems like. I think that because of the poor footing and the depth they had, we might have shown a little fatigue late in the game."

With 1:37 left, a Paul Toscano pass went through Washington's fingertips, was batted up in the air by a couple of LSU defenders and ended up in the hands of UW tight end George Anderson.

"When I saw Anderson running with the football I started running for my life," said Tigers defensive back Barton Frye, who pulled Anderson down at the LSU 18 after a 54-yard gain. "I don't know if I can run that fast again."

On what turned out to be the final play of the Sugar Bowl, Toscano completed a pass to Huey, who was dragged down by defensive back Gerry Kent at the 5.

Without any timeouts remaining, the clock ran out on Wyoming's perfect season.

"I would have given half a year's salary for 10 more seconds. Just 10 more seconds," Eaton lamented after the game. (1)

LSU 20, Wyoming 13.

"LSU played its best game and we did not play ours, at least in the second half," Eaton said. "I was real proud of our team. They came to play. They always do, though. All of us are proud of them."

Nels still believes the outcome of the game would have been different had he not been forced to watch in agony from the sideline.

"We should have won," Nels said nearly 40 years later. "I broke my ankle in the second quarter so I watched the second half from the bench. I remember it was cold and rainy, just a crappy day. We went into half leading 13-0 and ended up losing, but they weren't a better team."

Despite the loss, the Cowboys were ranked sixth in the final Associated Press poll and fifth by the UPI behind the likes of Southern California, Tennessee, Oklahoma and Notre Dame.

The national attention would help the coaches on the recruiting trail from coast to coast as they reloaded the roster for another run at a New Year's Day bowl.

"I watched them play in the Sugar Bowl when they had Jim Kiick and Jerry DePoyster and all those guys," said Lionel Grimes, who would join the program a year later after an all-state high school career in

Alliance, Ohio. "That's how I knew about Wyoming. I remember from watching the game on television that they had the Cowboy riding a bucking horse on the helmets and they wore gold pants and they played good football."

But not long after the Sugar Bowl, the party was over for Wyoming football.

During the 60s, Wyoming fans loved their Cowboys—black and white.

Although it was not a shock for any of the players from the south, Huey's eyes were opened quickly to how much progress still needed to be made on the civil rights front while on the trip to New Orleans.

"When we played in the Sugar Bowl, it was a shock to me because even at that time we went to a restaurant and the guy said he couldn't seat all of us because some of us were black," Huey said. "And what was also shocking was to go out on that field and see that LSU didn't have any blacks on their team or on the coaching staff. That was all a little bit of a shock to me."

Montgomery, a Cheyenne native who happens to be white, had a similar experience.

"We never thought about it when we went down there, but we had a guy in the band, a saxophone player named Morris Tate from Cheyenne, who was black," Montgomery said. "We had never thought about it, but we were down on Canal Street and went to go into a bar and they would not let him in. That was something that was really surprising because in Wyoming we never thought about that."

Soon enough, race and football would be on everyone's mind in the Equality State.

The Voice of Change

Mel Hamilton was paralyzed with fear, perhaps even in a state of shock after what had just taken place. Without warning, his mother had plucked him from the family home—where she raised him by herself along with his four brothers and six sisters—and dragged her son down to the bus stop.

Wearing a second-hand seersucker suit in the sweltering August heat and carrying a cream-colored suitcase and a bag of chicken sandwiches, Hamilton was sent away from his childhood home on the North Carolina coast to embark on a cross-country journey that would change the course of his life and the history of Wyoming football.

Hamilton was 14 years old. The year was 1961.

Five years earlier, Rosa Parks had bravely refused a bus driver's orders to give up her seat to a white passenger in Montgomery, Alabama. But all Hamilton was able to do was cry in his seat at the very back of the bus as it crawled through the south en route to parts of the country this wide-eyed teenager had only dreamt about.

"I had to go through deep Ku Klux Klan country. When we went through Tennessee, I was urinating on myself. I never raised my head and was scared as hell," Hamilton recalled. "I could see a lot of white kids about my age out the window when we stopped in some of the towns. About a day and a half after I left Wilmington, I finally forced myself to get off and cringed past those guys. I went to the black side of the bus station to use the restroom. I didn't have a change of clothes. I just tried to clean up the mess I had made."

Hamilton would spend four days and three nights on the bus before reaching his destination: Omaha, Nebraska. His mom had arranged for him to attend school at Boys Town, which was founded by Father Edward Flanagan in 1917 to care for and educate at-risk children of all races, colors and creeds.

"No race that does not take care of its young can hope to survive—or deserves to survive," Father Flanagan once said. (3)

It was in Boys Town where Mel Hamilton evolved into a man—a strong, athletic, political, black man. He was the type of young man whose voice would be heard in America during the 1960s.

When Hamilton finally, reluctantly, stepped off the bus in Omaha, there was no one to greet him. He had no instructions as to where to find the school. And no idea what his mother was getting him into.

After standing in silence for what felt like an eternity, he summoned up the courage to ask for directions to Boys Town and was quickly on his way to a new beginning.

Instead of segregation, Hamilton found himself immersed in diversity. He befriended a Navajo and they made a pact to watch each other's back and to fight for respect in their new community together. The school also included its share of Hispanic and Asian boys.

"It was the first time I had met someone who was not black or white," Hamilton said. "We saw things and people that we never thought we would. It was truly a place where harmony existed. That was the goodness of Boys Town . . . . But being in a special place like that is also a detriment. Because we left Boys Town thinking that the rest of the world was like that."

Two years into the program, Hamilton became a councilman for his cottage, representing the interests of 20 of his peers. Eventually he ran for and was elected mayor of Boys Town. When dignitaries like President

Gerald Ford or Harlem Globetrotter Meadowlark Lemon visited, the well-spoken 16-year-old was among the first to meet and greet them.

Initially, Hamilton refused overtures to play football at Boys Town. He was big enough, fast enough, and tough enough. But he simply didn't enjoy the sport.

Football, however, quickly became a part of Hamilton's life when he realized he could use it to further his education. It turns out he was as good on the gridiron as he was in the school's political arena.

Hamilton received scholarship offers from Cornell, Northwestern and Wyoming to play football. He said there may have been other opportunities, but "Boys Town only told you about letters where they wanted you to go."

Wyoming was Hamilton's third choice until his best friend, Ken Gilchrist, was also offered a scholarship to play football in Laramie.

"I only played the game of football because I was very good at it. But I never really enjoyed it," Hamilton said. "I forced myself to play well enough to get what I needed. Kenny didn't have anybody but me, so I chose to stay with him."

When Hamilton received his diploma from Boys Town, his mom and one of his sisters were there to witness the ceremony. His father had once again missed out on a memory.

Hamilton was born in Charleston, South Carolina, in 1947. His father had been a machinist in the city's harbor during World War II. Once the war was over, he left the family to use his carpentry and masonry skills wherever the work would take him.

Like too many young, black boys, Hamilton said "I saw very little of my father. Mom raised all of us kids. And I am what they call a 'knee baby.' Do you know what a knee baby is? That's the next-to-youngest child. The youngest is in the arms of the mother and the next-to-youngest is always on the mother's knee."

When the Hamilton 'knee baby' was three, the family moved to Wilmington, North Carolina, a beautiful port city many of the Confederate States had relied on to receive supplies during the American Revolution.

In 1865, the Union won the Battle of Wilmington and took control of the city. In 1898 over 100 blacks fell victim to the Wilmington Massacre—also know as the Wilmington Race Riot of 1898—an attempt by white supremacists opposed to the power held by all of the black and white elected officials in what was a predominately African-American city.

It is the only recorded coup d'état to occur on American soil. (4)

The Hamilton family, of course, lived in the "black section" of Wilmington. Mel attended St. Thomas, a small, all-black Catholic school that was about a mile's walk from the house.

On the way to school he walked silently past St. Mary's, the all-white Catholic school, save for one unforgettable afternoon on the diamond.

"Not once did we mingle until 1961 when the schools played a softball game," Hamilton said. "I loved it because of the fact we beat the snot out of them."

Hamilton was an alter boy but still afraid of the black nuns and he tried not to talk to the white priest. It was understood, even as a child, that a black person was not to make any waves or create any problems around a white person, especially one in a position of authority.

"Because of religion, mom never allowed us to bad-mouth white people," Hamilton said. "I don't know if she felt that way or if she just wanted to give us survival skills. We had seen fights and the Ku Klux

Klan. We all knew that racism existed. We knew 'our place.'

"I grew up being very afraid of white folks. And that didn't leave me until the Black 14."

The Eaton Way

Lloyd Eaton was as tough as the South Dakota prairie. He grew up on a rural farm about six miles east of Belle Fourche, South Dakota, just north of the Black Hills. His grandfather had purchased the rugged but beautiful plot of Western American soil on the new frontier after arriving in 1877.

Life on the farm was good but certainly not easy. Eaton was born on March 23, 1918, and worked hard to help his parents, Thomas and Rosa, during the Great Depression. The family used a horse and buggy or the old 1914 Ford Touring Car to get into town or for trips to nearby Spearfish, South Dakota.

"It was home and every kid worked," explained Eaton's sister, Doris Shipley, his only sibling, who now lives in Spearfish. "That was all there was to it. Lloyd took on chores and whatever was expected of a kid . . . . Dad was not a harsh disciplinarian, but what dad said was what you did. I don't think that's an unusual trait for most families."

Football provided an opportunity for Eaton to bond with his father, who had also played the game. Doris was away at college when her brother played for the high school team, but she heard stories of the young football legend. Eaton also had an impressive prep career on the track and in the boxing ring and was just as passionate about fishing and hunting.

In addition to the farm, Eaton's grandfather also bought a lot in Spearfish where he built a home so his family could have easier access to higher education. Black Hills Teachers College (now Black Hills State University) is located in Spearfish. Thomas, Rosa and Doris all earned college degrees. Eaton, after graduating from Belle Fourche High School in 1936, would do the same while also playing football for the BHTC Yellow Jackets.

"Mother was a teacher. I was expected to be a teacher and I was. It was expected, I guess, that we were all going to go to college," Doris said. "Lots of farm people did not go on to college. Our family was expected to have an education."

Doris' husband opened a service station in Belle Fourche that Eaton worked at during the summers while attending college. The family was able to watch most of Eaton's football games. He also participated in speech and drama, and prepared himself to get into coaching before graduating in 1940.

About a year after taking a coaching and teaching position in Dupree, South Dakota, Eaton's life—like everyone else's in his generation—was interrupted by World War II. He served in the Infantry, becoming a Captain before he was discharged at the close of the great conflict. Like most WWII veterans, Eaton didn't talk much about what happened during his time serving abroad, according to Shipley.

Once he returned from the war, Eaton coached for two years in Martin, South Dakota. He decided to go back to school and received his Master's Degree at the University of Michigan. After graduation in 1949, he coached at Alma (Michigan) College for several years, leading the Scots to a dazzling 40-20-2 record, including Michigan Intercollegiate Athletic Association champion- ships in 1950 and '51. He moved on to coach Northern Michigan State College in 1956, but only stayed for one year because he received a call from Bob Devaney.

The Wyoming head coach, who would later build a national power at Nebraska, offered Eaton a chance to be a part of his staff in Laramie as the defensive line coach.

During Eaton's five years as an assistant coach, Wyoming racked up a 35-10-5 record, including a victory over Hardin-Simmons University in the Sun Bowl on January 1, 1959. Then in 1962, when Devaney left for Nebraska, Eaton was named his successor.

Eaton had an intimidating presence during his days as the head coach at Wyoming. He was the program's version of Woody Hayes and Paul "Bear" Bryant—a larger than life figure whose control over the program was never questioned. The Cowboys became a well-oiled, winning machine after some frustrating late-season road losses spoiled his first couple seasons. In 1963, for example, the Cowboys posted a 2-0 conference mark at home, then lost three straight WAC games at Arizona, New Mexico and Arizona State.

Eaton knew he needed more speed on both sides of the ball. He found that type of athleticism in the form of black players like Gene Huey, Vic Washington, Tony McGee, LaVerne Dickinson, Dick Speights and Joe Williams, and white players like Dennis Devlin, Jim Barrows, Tom Silvanic and Jim Stankus.

After winning three consecutive WAC titles, Eaton was in complete control and pushing all of the right buttons.

The 1969 season began as more of the same. The Pokes opened the campaign with a comfortable victory over Arizona before facing some adversity on the road at Air Force. After falling behind by a large deficit at the intermission, the players in the visiting locker room at Falcon Stadium were expecting Eaton to barge in and let them have it.

"In that Air Force game in '69 we were getting our butt kicked in the first half. They were running all over us and they owned us," junior split end John Griffin said. "Eaton walks in and all he has to do is look at you with a certain look and you know you better get your act together. He just said, 'Gentlemen, you know what you've got to do.'

"And instantly guys' eyes changed. We came out and just annihilated them. The final score was close, but we came back and blew them away."

Wyoming won the game 27-25.

The word that best described Eaton's philosophy of coaching was: Discipline. Every player who put on a

Wyoming uniform from 1957 to 1970 understood it was a part of Eaton's DNA.

In order for the Cowboys to win WAC championships and receive bids to bowl games, they had to adhere to the coach's strict rules on and off the field. It was understood that you did not step out of line in this program. It was the Eaton way.

The championship teams of 1966, '67 and '68 thrived under the team concept.

"Lloyd was a strict disciplinarian and anything you were involved with that requires teamwork had to require discipline," Gene Huey said. "I had discipline in my life ever since I could remember, so it was not a problem with me . . . .

"(Eaton) was a guy who ran the ship and did a good job at it at that time. He was a good football coach. But he wanted everything done the right way. You can have all kinds of talent, but without discipline you will not win."

During the late 60s, many male college students wore their hair long and grew beards or moustaches. It was also a time when a lot of young people experimented with drug use.

The Wyoming locker room looked as clean-cut as it did in the 50s. The only difference was the players were getting bigger, stronger and faster, and some of the faces in the team picture were black.

"Coach Eaton didn't even want you to have a shadow of a moustache or anything," McGee said.

Paul Roach, the top offensive assistant, said the talented staff Eaton assembled meshed perfectly under his leadership during the glory days.

"We had a good relationship. In a group setting there's always going to be some different personalities, but it was a good group of coaches and they all worked very hard and got along quite well," Roach said. "So it became pretty productive. A lot of that was influenced by the head coach. He was a very strong disciplinarian, although he did give us quite a bit of room for innovation and responsibility."

Eaton would not listen to the advice of his top lieutenants when the social war between coach's discipline and players' constitutional rights collided in October of 1969.

"Fellas . . . You're Through"

Laramie, Wyoming, was an idyllic place to be throughout the 1960s. For the most part, all was quiet in the sleepy college town—unless there was a home football game going on at War Memorial Stadium.

Nestled between the breathtaking vistas of the Snowy Range to the west and the granite and pine covered Laramie Mountains to the east, Laramie sits at 7,220 feet on the high plains of southeastern Wyoming.

And up in the crisp, thin air, the young voices of change that were screaming to be heard across the country during the volatile decade didn't echo over the mountains and into the Gem City.

"In the 1960s, a lot of things were going on with civil rights—the black fists at the '68 Olympics in Mexico, protesting the war in Vietnam, and there were a lot of things going on at campuses across the country with Black Student Alliances," Gene Huey said. "And Wyoming being where it was isolated, things don't hit there as fast. But eventually they do come."

Meanwhile, outside the isolation . . . .

Muhammad Ali was the heavyweight champion of the world and an enemy of the state. He dodged the draft like a butterfly and stung his opponents like a bee. He was strong. He was black. And he would be heard.

Ali remains The Greatest today, but in the 1960s he was at his most colorful in a black and white America going through a social revolution.

Soldiers were dying in Vietnam, and college students were protesting on campus. One of the strongest voices was that of the black athlete.

Not at the University of Wyoming.

The only colors that mattered here in the '60s were brown and gold, and the only issue worth paying attention to was Cowboy football.

"As far as I was concerned, that was the golden age of football," recalls UW sports information director Kevin McKinney, who was a freshman on the Laramie campus in 1967. "Wyoming was in a mode at that time that any loss was devastating. We were used to winning." (5)

The program won in the '50s under Bob Devaney, who would leave to become a legend at Nebraska, and it was starting to win big in the '60s under Lloyd Eaton.

In 1966, UW finished 10-1, including a 28-20 victory over Florida State in the Sun Bowl. The Cowboys' only loss came at Colorado State when the

Rams quarterback bounced a lateral to the running back who pretended to be disgusted and then threw a touchdown pass.

In 1967, the team was 10-1 again, with its only loss coming in the Sugar Bowl on New Year's Day 1968 in front of a national television audience.

Many felt the Cowboys had their best team in 1969, and a 4-0 start backed it up.

And then it happened. Race, religion, authority, protest and football collided on these high plains.

On Friday, October 17, 1969, the 14 black athletes on the UW team entered coach Eaton's office wearing black armbands. They wanted to do something in support of the Black Student Alliance's efforts in Laramie and show solidarity with the national movment. They wanted to talk to the coach about possibly wearing the armbands during the upcoming game against Brigham Young University to protest the Mormon Church's policy prohibiting blacks from holding the priesthood.

As soon as he saw them enter his office, Eaton ushered the 14 players into the upper bleachers of the Fieldhouse and informed them they were all off the team.

Suddenly, the school colors had changed from brown and gold to black vs. white.

They had come from as far away as Massachusetts and California, from southern cities such as Chattanooga, Tennessee; Pine Bluff, Arkansas; and Wilmington, North Carolina; from football hotbeds like Michigan and Texas, and one of them from nearby Hanna, Wyoming.

They were the 14 black football players who had come to Laramie for the 1969 season. Although most of them never became famous and all of them are infamous in Wyoming, the Black 14 made a lasting impact on the program and became an important part of the Equality State's civil rights history.

The names of the Black 14 should be remembered: **Jerry Berry, Tony Gibson, John Griffin, Lionel Grimes, Mel Hamilton, Ron Hill, Willie Hysaw, Jim Isaac, Earl Lee, Tony McGee, Don Meadows, Ivie Moore, Joe Williams, Ted Williams.**

What would turn out to be a raging wildfire by the end of the week began on October 13, 1969, the Monday following the Cowboys' 39-7 victory over Texas-El Paso, when Willie Black, the chancellor of UW's Black Student Alliance, informed members of the group about policies in the Church of Jesus Christ of Latter-Day Saints that prohibited blacks from ascending to the priesthood.

Black informed the players that BYU, set to play in Laramie five days later, was funded by the Mormon Church.

"Willie came on campus and he started doing research based on our complaints. He found out that blacks could not be priests and about blacks suffering other insults from the Mormon Church, which ran BYU," said Hamilton, one of the most vocal of the Black 14. "We thought that we had to do something about it. Students were expressing their rights all over the country." (5)

There were student protests surrounding BYU's visits to other WAC campuses before and after the Black 14 incident at Wyoming.

On October 16, Black sent letters to the university officials at Wyoming and BYU, members of the media, the WAC commissioner, the president of the Mormon Church and Eaton asking that UW refuse the use of its athletic facilities to host BYU and that athletic directors in the conference refuse to schedule games with BYU as long as the Mormon Church continued its racist policies.

After Wyoming's practice on Thursday, Joe Williams, a black tri-captain, met with Eaton and told the coach that the 14 black players wanted to wear black armbands during the game against BYU as a protest of the Mormon Church's policies, which they interpreted as racist.

Eaton told Williams he would not allow it. The coach's initial view: If the black players had a problem with the way they were treated by BYU, then they should take it out on them on the football field.

"There was a lot of trash-talk in the previous games against BYU," Hamilton, an offensive lineman, said. "They used a lot of racial slurs. They had gone on Mormon missions, so they were two or three years older, but we weren't afraid of them because we beat them. But we didn't like being called niggers and getting cheap shots."

During separate interviews nearly 40 years after their UW playing days had abruptly ended, a number of the players brought up an anecdote about the grounds crew at BYU turning on the sprinklers immediately after games against Wyoming in Provo—before the Cowboys had a chance to get off the field.

"It was brewing because we kept thinking about playing BYU and why they always turned the water on us," Lee said. "They wanted to wash the demons off the field and cleanse the field as soon as possible. That began to irritate people, especially young people. Just because we were football players doesn't mean we weren't aware of what was going on. And we wanted to stand up and do something about it."

Hours after Eaton had denied Joe Williams' request, the black players met in a dormitory to discuss the situation. They still wanted to wear the armbands and would do so inside the coach's office in an attempt to persuade him to change his mind and allow them to go forward with what they viewed as a harmless, silent protest.

The group did not intend to make any demands of the head coach.

"Students on the campus were planning a demonstration against the Mormon policies, and we voted that we would take part in that demonstration. And our part was wearing black armbands, if coach Eaton would let us," Gibson recalled. "If Eaton didn't let us, we would just play the game. That's the part that was never brought out enough after the fact."

Some of the veteran players warned those in the group who were either married or new to the program that the situation could turn ugly.

"When we were walking to Eaton's office, Jerome Berry asked me, 'Do you think he's going to put us off the team?'" McGee said. "I said, 'Yes, I do.'"

Hamilton said he had witnessed a darker side of Eaton a few years earlier when he told the coach that he was planning to get married to a white woman.

"(Athletic director) Red Jacoby said, 'That's great Mel.' He thought it was a good idea to settle down," Hamilton said. "But Eaton said, 'Oh, hell no. I can't let you marry a white girl with the people of Wyoming's money.'

"He said the people of Casper (Wyoming) would not allow me to let you do this. I never knew where Casper was and I got angry and had to be talked out of dropping out of school."

Hamilton did not end up marrying the girl and volunteered for the Army following the 1966 season. After 18 months of service, he returned to the team with Eaton's blessing.

"That was more a reflection of my football skills than Eaton's remorse," Hamilton said. "I came back more mature, I didn't let things excite me. I used every bit of that time in the Army as reflection. I came back as somewhat of a leader." (5)

The outspoken Hamilton, however, would not lead the discussion with the head coach on the darkest Friday in Wyoming football history.

There was no debate.

As soon as the players showed up at his door wearing the armbands, the rash decision on the issue had been made.

Eaton, who thought he had made it perfectly clear to Joe Williams that wearing the black armbands, on or off the field of play, was breaking team rules, escorted the players into the Fieldhouse and got right to the point as the players sat in silence in the front rows of the upper bleachers.

"He took us all into the bleachers and the first thing he said was, 'Fellas, I'm going to save you a lot of time and trouble: You're through. As of now you are no longer Wyoming Cowboy football players,'" Hamilton recalled.

The moment, dubbed "the Black 14" incident by the media, changed Wyoming football history and the lives of everyone involved forever.

"This is strictly a disciplinary issue," is how Eaton explained his startling decision to the press. "The players to me are Cowboys, and their color does not have any bearing on it." (6)

The 14 players didn't say much as they left the surreal meeting with Eaton.

"We were all kids—18, 19, 20 years old," Lee said. "Some guys didn't fully understand the impact of what was happening, and once the ball started rolling it all happened so fast."

Some of the players were stunned at the racial slurs Eaton had thrown in their faces. Some were stunned that their promising football careers had just ended. Some assumed the athletic director or the university president or the governor would right the wrong and get them reinstated. Some were scared about what the reaction would be from the other students, the fans and the media.

And some were simply lost as they limped out of the one-sided meeting.

"I was disillusioned when the Black 14 happened," Hamilton said. "We were angry and most of us needed a day off to lick our wounds. We reminded each other that everyone was polarized on campus and to be careful of certain groups. A lot of people were concerned about safety. I was feeling a little uncomfortable."

Eaton then told Jacoby about his decision. Jacoby informed UW president William Carlson. And Jacoby and Carlson met that afternoon with the 14 black players without the head coach.

Phil White, the editor of the student newspaper, *The Branding Iron*, rushed over to the president's office and sat in on the session after hearing about Eaton's dismissal in the Student Union.

"What was really disappointing to me, with so much riding on understanding these players and where they were coming from, all of the leaders—from the state, the university, the athletic department—had no conception of what was going on in these players' minds," White said. "No one had made any effort to understand how they might relate to the civil rights struggle which had been going on for years before that."

The players wanted to meet with all of the coaches to try and explain their point of view. The requested meeting did not take place. Later, Eaton told the University leaders, who he was supposed to be working for, that the 14 could meet with him individually to discuss possible reinstatement.

Meanwhile, Jerry Hollon, the President of the UW Board of Trustees, called an emergency meeting of the board for that Friday evening. The meeting lasted from about 8 p.m. until 3:30 a.m. with no resolution.
Governor Stan Hathaway, an attorney and an ex-officio member of the board, drove through a wicked snowstorm from Cheyenne to Laramie, determined to resolve the conflict.

"The meetings were all directed toward trying to convince us to change our minds," Hamilton said. "They said, 'Don't throw your lives away,' and that they had given us a chance to get out of the ghetto, even though most of us weren't from the ghetto. If they would have forced Eaton to the table that night, something would have been worked out. The trustees were saying it was our fault, that they would not negotiate and their minds were made up." (5)

Coach Eaton's regular practice was to take the team to a movie on Friday nights before a home game. At one point during the trustees meeting, Carlson went to the movie theater downtown and called Eaton out of the movie to ask him to come to the trustees meeting. Eaton refused. Later in the meeting, Carlson and Hathaway went to Eaton's home and talked to him there.

The 14 players did go to the meeting as requested, but they had no legal representation. Many of them were minors under the law at that time.

The upshot of it all was that the powers that be in the state of Wyoming sided with Eaton. According to Hathaway, when asked in the wee hours if they would play against BYU without the armbands, some of the 14 indicated that they would not and that they also would not play for Eaton again.

"The black students told Dr. Carlson and myself they could not play in the football game with Brigham Young without wearing black armbands," Hathaway said. "Several of the students also stated they would not play football for the University of Wyoming if Lloyd Eaton remained as coach. Under these circumstances, the president and the board of trustees had no alternative other than to support coach Eaton in his decision to dismiss the protesting team members." (7)

The 14 black players remember the meeting differently. They say they were booted from the program for merely asking the head football coach if they could express themselves politically on campus in 1969, not demanding it.

"Coach Eaton was a Bobby Knight before Bobby Knight's era. It was his rule or no rule," Lee said. "In fact, at that time his authority superseded the university president's authority. He was in charge of the campus. He truly believed that he ruled the university and what he said was gold."

On Saturday, October 18, a suddenly all-white Wyoming team dismantled the usual all-white BYU team 40-7 in front of a standing room only crowd at War Memorial Stadium.

In the October 19 edition of the *Laramie Boomerang,* hall of fame sports writer Larry Birleffi accurately captured the pro-Eaton sentiments that echoed from the stands that afternoon with these words: *They'll be back, and not as blacks or whites, or pinks or blues, but together as Americans instilled with the pride of playing Cowboy football. (8)*

Outside the gates, a handful of protesters showed up to participate in the Black Students Alliance demonstration. Police confiscated their placards as they entered the stadium for the game. As the game was winding down, the crowd of 14,993 roared, "We love Eaton! We love Eaton! We love Eaton!"

Several of the Black 14 bravely attended the game and sat in the stands watching their former teammates. They couldn't help but notice a man in the top row of the stadium waving a large confederate flag.

"I said to a police officer, 'What about this flag up there?'" *Branding Iron* Editor White said. "He said: 'Free speech.'

"I was sad and really devastated because up to that point I had had such a great regard for the University of Wyoming. I just couldn't believe something like this would happen."

Annie Marie Walthall, a 49-year-old UW employee who regularly walked in the Fieldhouse for exercise, stated in a 1997 UW documentary that she was able to see and hear Eaton as he spoke to the players above in the bleachers. She said he paced back and forth and spoke loudly.

"It was pretty belligerent talk," Walthall said. "I felt embarrassed that the young men were hearing this tirade." (9)

Soon after their dismissal, the Black 14 began looking for an attorney to represent them. According to Willie Black, they were turned down by Gerry Spence, who even then had a reputation as an extraordinary trial attorney in Wyoming. They then contacted Cheyenne lawyer Chuck Graves and he agreed to represent them, knowing full well that doing so would win him few friends among the Wyoming populace.

"The leadership in the state in effect let the coach call the shots and the net result was the total devastation of the university program and the image of the university," Graves said. "My interest was in achieving a compromise but the attitude of the state throughout was, 'it's Lloyd Eaton's way or no way.'" (9)

After the meeting with Eaton in which they were dismissed from the team, the 14 black players took the uniforms from their lockers and piled them in the center of the room.

Then they walked from the Fieldhouse to the Student Union. When they arrived, word had already spread about the incident.

"By the time we got to the Union, a student met us at the front door and he said, 'I hear you guys are boycotting the team,'" Griffin said. "I said: 'We just got kicked off the team.'

"The spin was on that fast. We probably walked slowly from the Fieldhouse, but it was within a half hour of the meeting."

When asked to explain his reasoning for removing the 14 black players from his team, Eaton told state and university officials that the group had violated two team rules:

1. That players will not form themselves into groups of factions but act as individuals.
2. That players will not participate in student demonstrations of any kind.

Eaton's second rule could easily be viewed as unconstitutional by the U.S. Supreme Court in *Tinker vs. Des Moines Independent Community School District* decided February 24, 1969, the court ruled that a high school student's expulsion from school for wearing an arm band in protest of the Vietnam War was unconstitutional. (10)

Two days later Eaton modified the second rule, permitting players to demonstrate so long as it was not on the playing field.

"(Eaton) could have worked out a deal to suspend us for the BYU game, we were too tired to play anyway after being at the trustees meeting until the early hours, and reinstate us the next week. We could have salvaged the season and resolved the issue," Griffin said. "But he was a pretty arrogant guy and Cowboy football was the No. 1 most important thing in the state. I didn't realize that Cowboy football was such a strong piece of Wyoming until the incident . . . .

"We were going against Eaton and Cowboy football, so he took offense and everyone supported him."

Almost everyone.

On October 18, the day after the Black 14 was dismissed by Eaton, the University of Wyoming Student Senate held an emergency meeting and passed a resolution condemning the coach's actions: . . . *the Student Senate expresses its shock at the callous, insensitive treatment afforded 14 black athletes who acted on a matter of conscience with restraint, with moderation, and with responsibility.* (7)

White wrote an editorial in *The Branding Iron* that appeared the following Friday, siding with the players. He received so much flack for the opinion that he decided to step down from his position the following week and focus on finishing law school at UW.

"I wrote an editorial saying they were kicked off the team for violating rules, these rules have now been rescinded and by all rights the players should be put back on the team," White recalled. "The state rallied behind the coach . . . . It was a tragedy for the players.

I'm sure they suffered a great deal. And Eaton is a tragic figure. He essentially ruined his own life and I feel partly responsible because I was involved in this deification previously as a sports writer. I remember writing all these glowing articles about him for the paper, including an article about how a big part of his success was the discipline he required of his players."

On December 1, 1969, the UW chapter of the American Association of University Professors drafted and signed a belated memorandum to Carlson stating their support of the Black 14.

The specific rights involved in the incident of October 17 are those to free expression and the freedom to support causes by orderly means. These rights are necessary to the university and to the development of its students in the pursuit by both of the general well-being of society. Of course free expression is indispensable to the educational process. (10)

By October 20, the Monday after the BYU game, the national press corps marched into Laramie, not to write articles about the undefeated and nationally ranked Pokes, but to focus on the 14 players who were suddenly no longer a part of the program.

Eaton told United Press International (UPI) that he "wouldn't be surprised" if UW released him from his contract.

"But you know damned well I'm not gonna quit," he said. (11)

In an editorial published the Sunday after the BYU game, *The Denver Post* challenged the citizens of Wyoming to contest their coach: *For a coach at the University of Wyoming or elsewhere to issue an edict that football players may not take part on their own time in a lawful Vietnam demonstration or may not protest policies they think are racist at Brigham Young University is an outrage.*

It is to suggest that football players are less than human and that they can be deprived of rights which the Constitution of the United States guarantees to other American citizens.

The power of the State of Wyoming ought not to be used by a football coach or anyone else to defy the Constitution. And all coaches should be made to understand that the dictatorship they exercise in athletic matters cannot extend to politics.

If Coach Lloyd Eaton cannot accept that, then it is he, and not his 14 black players, who should leave the team.

Winning football, to which Eaton has contributed more than his share, is important in Wyoming. But it is more important than human rights? We hope not, and we hope the people of Wyoming, on and off the campus, will prove that it is not. (12)

On October 25, San Jose State's players wore multi-colored armbands in support of the Black 14 during a game at War Memorial Stadium.

After Wyoming's 16-7 victory, *Sports Illustrated's* Pat Putnam wrote: *Oh, it was a beautiful homecoming. The weather was as pretty as the queen, cool and crisp, and nobody minded a little wind. As people strolled from the stadium last Saturday they laughed and talked about how their unbeaten Wyoming had just man-handled San Jose State 16-7, which made it hard to get up a real working anger against those 14 black athletes Coach Lloyd Eaton threw off the team two weeks ago. Coach Eaton had shown those protesters he could win without them. Good riddance, and never mind a lot of talk about civil rights, because this is Wyoming, and out here we do things our way. Like Coach Eaton told those athletes: Boys, if you don't like the way we run things around here then you better go play at Grambling or Morgan State. Yes sir, and wasn't that victory over San Jose State just glorious?*

"Yes, it was a glorious victory," said Bill Waterman, smiling thinly, "and now we shall see about the rest." Waterman is an NAACP lawyer out of Detroit, a short, rather round, quiet-spoken man, and he arrived in Laramie, Wyoming, last week with the belief that the rights of a student should not be limited just because he is an athlete. His first move will be to seek an injunction against the University of Wyoming in federal court this week. "First we want to get the players reinstated," he said. "Then we'll go from there." (13)

On October 29, a civil lawsuit, "Williams vs. Eaton," was filed in U.S. District Court in Cheyenne on behalf of the Black 14, naming the State of Wyoming, the Board of Trustees, Jacoby, Carlson and Eaton as defendants and seeking $1.1 million in damages. An injunction was also sought in Cheyenne to reinstate the players, but that was quickly denied by U.S. District Judge Ewing T. Kerr.

All of the players were present in the Cheyenne courtroom for a hearing on November 10, but only one member of the Black 14, Hamilton, was present throughout the long, painful legal process.

"I imagine there were people in that group who were not ready for that fight. You've got to know yourself and you have to be ready to fight," Hamilton said. "That was my right of passage . . . . The judge just laughed at our lawyer from Detroit (Waterman) and called him boy and used derogatory comments. We felt it was a sham and a kangaroo court.

"As the years went by I found myself alone in front of the judge. That was a lonely feeling."

On November 17, 1969, judge Ewing Kerr entered an order denying the Black 14's application for a temporary restraining order restoring them to the team. The Black 14 therein filed their notice of appeal to the U.S. 10th Circuit Court of Appeals.

On March 25, 1970, Kerr dismissed the case. On May 14, 1972, the U.S. 10th Circuit Court of Appeals in Denver supported the lower court's decision to dismiss.

The Black 14 did not seek to appeal to the U.S. Supreme Court.

On June 9, 1978, Spencer W. Kimball, the president of the Mormon Church, received a revelation from God and changed church policy to provide that worthy black male members of the church may hold the priesthood.

"I've never told anyone this," Hamilton said with a smile during a 1999 interview with a reporter. "My oldest son became a Mormon. I know my son, who experimented with several religions, agonized over this decision and he was very concerned I would be upset. He and I never really sat down and talked about the Black 14 . . . .

"Now when I think, 'Did I make it possible for him to choose this religion?' The answer is yes. Now he has the strength to join something I fought against. And that is what it was all about." (5)

The Other Side of the Locker Room

Larry "Bo" Nels was an important recruit for Wyoming. So much so that Lloyd Eaton personally made the long trip from Laramie to North Syracuse, New York, to make sure the Cowboys landed the powerful defensive lineman.

"That was the nicest Eaton ever was to me," Nels said when asked about his first impression of Eaton. "He was a tough guy. He was no-nonsense and very strict. But as long as you stayed out of trouble, there weren't any problems."

There certainly weren't any problems for the Cowboys on fall Saturdays. Nels arrived at UW in 1966 just as the program started piling up WAC championship trophies. He was a herculean presence in the defensive line.

"The years I was there, we never lost a home game. That was special," said Nels, who quickly emerged as one of the greatest defensive players in the program's history and an anchor on the nation's top-ranked defense in 1967. "Winning a WAC championship is nice. Now days if you win a conference championship, they give you a big ring, not back then. It was just kind of expected of us."

As a senior in 1969, Nels expected another conference title and perhaps a perfect season for the Pokes.

"We had a great team. If we didn't go undefeated we probably would have lost maybe one game," Nels said. "What happened was shocking and so discouraging. It's still hard to believe it went down like that."

The Black 14 incident obviously changed everything for the black players and tarnished Eaton's coaching career and legacy. But the dramatic turn of events also had a devastating impact on the white Wyoming players, especially seniors like Nels.

After a 6-0 start, the nationally-ranked Cowboys faded down the stretch with lopsided losses at Arizona State, Utah, New Mexico and Houston.

"It was over in a hurry," Nels said. "We ran out of gas and we ran out of players. I remember my last game was very discouraging when we were beaten badly by Houston in the Astrodome."

Nels and Tommy Tucker were (the other) tri-captains on the team along with Joe Williams, who was kicked out of the program with the other 13 black players.

The Black 14 didn't communicate with the white players about their plan before going to the head coach, and the two sides didn't speak much after Eaton made his decision.

"I was in shock afterwards. As you look back you just wonder what could have been done differently and if a compromise could have been reached to appease Coach's strict rules," Nels said. "Maybe a one-game suspension or something, I don't know, but we didn't have any say in the matter. What Eaton said went."

Nels, an all-WAC selection in 1969, was supposed to play in the Senior Bowl and the Hula Bowl after the 1969 season to showcase his skills for pro scouts, but his name was removed from the rosters of the all-star games following the Black 14 incident.

"The scuttlebutt was they didn't want anyone from Wyoming because they thought there would be protests or controversy," Nels said.

The events caused Nels' draft stock to go down, but he was still selected by the New York Giants in the 12th round.

"I never lost respect for (Eaton)," Nels said. "I just felt bad for a lot of the guys for what happened, and for the seniors, too. We put in four years of hard work and we really wanted not only to win the WAC again but go to another big bowl game."

Nels still keeps in contact with stars from the Sugar Bowl team like Mike Dirks, Jim Kiick and Paul Toscano. The group gets together for reunions every few years. He also calls or emails senior classmates from the 1969 team like Al Zerfoss and Larry Suganuma on a weekly basis.

However, most of the Black 14 seemed to disappear after the incident in the eyes of those who were still playing Wyoming football.

"Afterwards I talked to a few of them, but most of them just wanted to get out of there," Nels said. "I didn't see them around. We were so busy going to class and football practice . . . . Ultimately, coach Eaton was the one who was hard-headed and he was going to do it his way. I don't think anybody could have talked him out of it."

It was not easy being a football player at Brigham Young in the 1960s. Early in the decade, there was a lot of losing, and during the latter part of the decade there was a lot of controversy.

"It was very emotional," recalled Tommy Hudspeth, who became a head coach for the first time at BYU in 1964. "You had to be guarded. Our players were very alert and they had worrisome times because they never knew what was going to happen. But they represented the school very well."

The Cougars were targets of protest before the Black 14 incident, and road trips to El Paso, Albuquerque, Tempe and even Fort Collins were extremely difficult and even dangerous for BYU athletes in the years that followed.

During an Arizona-BYU basketball game on January 8, 1970, a "near riot" occurred at Bear Down Gym in Tucson. Eight students were arrested in a melee that resulted in injuries to university policemen and college officials. A group of demonstrators forced their way onto the court which resulted in a 10-minute brawl. (14)

A little over a week later, during a wrestling competition against BYU, students of Colorado State

College (now the University of Northern Colorado) in Greeley, Colorado, sat on the mats after the national anthem in protest of the Mormon Church policies they viewed as racist. The police informed the gym crowd that they had been notified of a bomb threat at the gym. After the gym was emptied, the meet was held two hours later behind closed doors. (15)

When Colorado State hosted BYU for a men's basketball game, university officials denied a student request to protest at halftime of the February 5, 1970, game in support of the Black 14. Before the game started, 18 students linked arms at the south end of the court. Just prior to the game's opening tip, approximately 55 blacks carried placards that read: "End Racism in the W.A.C." (16)

The blacks marched onto the court with clenched fist salutes. The game included several stoppages due to eggs being thrown on the floor. And at halftime the blacks went back onto the court during the baton-twirling activities of the Cougarettes, prompting a clash with Fort Collins policemen equipped with helmets and nightsticks. A *Rocky Mountain News* photographer was injured by something thrown from the stands, leaving him unconscious on the floor and bleeding. (17)

Hudspeth led BYU to its first conference football championship in 1965. That season the Cougars pulled off impressive road wins at Arizona State (24-6), at Arizona (20-3) and at New Mexico (42-8) en route to the WAC title, but lost 34-6 in Laramie.

"The fans there . . . I'll never forget we were walking toward the stadium and everybody was tail-gating and they knew who we were," Hudspeth said of his first visit to Wyoming. "And everybody stopped us and wished us luck. They were very competitive, proud alumni and they came there to honor and support the school and to show that they were good. And they were."

Hudspeth was 0-6 against Wyoming from 1964-69 as the Cougars struggled to solve Fritz Shurmur's dominant defenses.

"They were just very aggressive, very alert, and well prepared. They had a great attitude about competition," Hudspeth said. "They'd line up and rattle your head, but it never crossed the line. You never had to worry about these people because their standards were extremely high."

Hudspeth said that before the infamous game on October 18, 1969, Eaton told him that he had kicked the 14 black players off the Wyoming team out of respect for BYU.

"Lloyd Eaton was one of the finest men I have ever known. He was not only a fine man but a fine football coach," said Hudspeth, who is Mormon. "He had the greatest of ethics. And he supported what I was trying to do at that time at BYU . . . . Lloyd told me about what was going on and said it was out of respect for us. It helped us establish everything and complete the program we were in the process of building. He showed the support he had for BYU, for the conference and for individuals. It was a big step."

Ironically, the dismissal of the Black 14 at UW helped open the door for the first black football player at BYU a year later. Hudspeth, an Oklahoma native who played at the University of Tulsa, recruited Ron Knight from the Sooner State to become the first black football player in BYU history in 1970.

"Ron was the one that took the brunt of what we were trying to do in regards to breaking the color lines," Hudspeth said. "Ron was quite a young man. He could handle everything. If you had to select someone to represent your school and your team, you would select someone like Ron. He wanted to do things right and he was proud of his race. He was put under the gun quite a few times and he came out right because he was quite a man."

Hudspeth, whose best move at BYU was hiring a brilliant, young assistant by the name of LaVell Edwards, finally defeated Eaton in 1970 as the Cougars beat Wyoming 23-3 in Provo. BYU also defeated Shurmur's Cowboys 35-17 in Laramie, but Hudspeth resigned as head coach after a 5-6 record in 1971. He would later become interim head coach at UTEP and of the Detroit Lions.

"If I ever had to make a choice of someone to play for it would be Lloyd. He was that kind of individual," Hudspeth, who has returned to Tulsa to help his alma mater with fundraising, said 40 years after Eaton's dynasty started to crumble. "I had Fritz Shurmur on my staff with the Detroit Lions. Fritz was an outstanding man and an outstanding football coach . . . . I've always felt very comfortable with Wyoming and had great respect for Wyoming because of the way the players handled themselves and competed."

After Hudspeth stepped down, Edwards took over and compiled a 257-101-3 record at BYU with 20 conference titles, including 10 consecutive WAC championships from 1976-85, and a national championship in 1984.

"I think '65 showed it could be done and that gave everybody a relaxed feeling. Then when we brought Ronnie in, and that opened the door for our recruiting," Hudspeth said. "I'm so proud of LaVell. I just want to hug his neck every time I see him."

Since the 1970 season, BYU's record against Wyoming is 28-7. And Cowboys fans, mostly because of what happened at UW in 1969, consider the now one-sided series a heated rivalry.

Opening the Door

The first official University of Wyoming football season was in 1893 and consisted of one game, a 14-0 victory over Cheyenne High School.

Former U.S. Senator Alan Simpson's stories about the Cowboys don't go back quite that far, but his father, Milward Simpson, was a halfback at UW from 1917-20 and passed his gridiron tales on to his sons.

"In those days, when they wore their helmets they were the kind you could roll up and put in your back pocket," Alan Simpson said. "Dad lived to be 95 and he just said it was a great experience. He was the captain of the football team, the baseball team and the basketball team."

When Milward Simpson was the president of the UW Board of Trustees, he was instrumental in the hiring of George "Duke" Humphrey as the university president and Glenn "Red" Jacoby as the athletic director. They brought in Bowden Wyatt as the head coach, and the modern era of Cowboy football began with a bang shortly after World War II.

The Cowboys only had 13 winning seasons in the first 50 years of the program and posted a 106-203-17 record from 1893-1946. UW had 15 coaches during that span and was known as a basketball school with Kenny Sailors leading the Pokes to an NCAA title in 1943 with his revolutionary jump shot.

The tide started to change dramatically in 1949 when Wyatt guided the Cowboys to a 9-1 record and construction began on the $750,000 War Memorial Stadium.

UW opened "The War" on September 23, 1950, with a 7-0 victory over Baylor in front of a crowd of 17,268.

"The Denver papers gave a lot more coverage to Wyoming at that time because it was the only team that had really developed in the region," said Doug Reeves, a two-way lineman for UW on the 1950 team. (18)

Behind the deep and powerful backfield of Eddie "Boom Boom" Talboom, Harry Geldien, Royal McMullen and John Melton, the Cowboys finished the 1950 season with a 10-0 record, including a 20-7 victory over Washington and Lee in the Gator Bowl.

UW finished ranked No. 12 in the Associated Press poll and No. 14 in the United Press International poll.

Alan Simpson was a freshman on the '50 squad and earned a varsity letter in '52 as a member of Wyatt's last UW team. It was a time of celebration on campus.

"One night we all went down to the American Legion club, about 15 or 20 of us. We decided we needed to drink a little beer to get the fluid back in us," Simpson said, with a laugh. "The team trainer was in there and it looked to us like he had passed out on the bar. His elbows were on the bar and he had his head in his hands. But later we found out that he was looking under his elbows to see who was there and then reported it to Wyatt.

"The next day at practice Wyatt said, 'Will all of the Legionnaires please step forward. You're going to run until you puke. When you are finished, you're going to take a coach to show him where you puked.'

"It was terrible. But you can bet that we didn't get caught drinking beer again."

Wyatt compiled a 39-17-1 record at UW before moving on and eventually turning his alma mater, Tennessee, into a national power.

Phil Dickens replaced Wyatt in 1953 and was 29-11-1 during his four seasons in Laramie, including a victory over Texas Tech in the Sun Bowl following the 1955 season. In 1956, the Cowboys had a perfect 10-0 season that was capped with a 7-6 victory at BYU.

Bob Devaney was 35-10-5 from 1957-61, including a victory over Hardin-Simmons in the 1958 Sun Bowl.

After Devaney left for Nebraska, Lloyd Eaton's record as head coach from 1962 until the Black 14 incident was 54-20-2. His record after kicking the 14 black players off the team in 1969 prior to the BYU game was 3-13.

"The sad one was the Black 14," Simpson said. "That didn't have to take place and it ruined Wyoming football for about 15 years . . . . It was very sad. Eaton was totally inflexible. He even made a couple racist remarks to one of the kids and they were stunned. Eaton never came back, even when the Sugar Bowl team was inducted into the (UW Athletics) Hall of Fame.

He must have been a bitter man. I don't know if he was, but I think he must have been."

Dave Christensen did a lot of homework before deciding to become the head coach at Wyoming on December 1, 2008. He didn't study the Black 14.

"I knew about the success that Paul Roach had there and Joe Tiller had," Christensen said. "I know they've had a lot of success in the past even further back. But I'm interested in the present time."

Christensen, who played for Don James at Washington in the early 80s and coached as an assistant under Gary Pinkel for 18 years, is a throwback in terms of the discipline he demands from today's players.

"A lot of the principles are the same as far as discipline, attention to detail, and the structure of the program," Christensen said when asked how similar his approach is to his old-school mentors. "We don't let things slide, we hold our players accountable, and there are no excuses."

Our society and culture have changed dramatically since Eaton adhered to a similar philosophy in Laramie. For starters, an African-American was elected president in 2008. "I didn't think I'd live to see it," Mel Hamilton said.

Nationally, college football is more popular than ever and the color that seems to matter the most is green. Head coaches earn seven-figure salaries at most of the prominent programs, and television money dictates scheduling and drives the controversial Bowl Championship Series.

Due to the high stakes, it's hard to imagine a coach anywhere sabotaging his own career by kicking 14 of his best players off the team for wanting to express themselves politically. Most coaches just tell the players not to post anything stupid or embarrassing on social networking Web sites like Facebook and Twitter.

The reality of recruiting in major college football today is that many of the top prep prospects choose schools based on facilities, playing time, television exposure and the coach's track record for sending players to the NFL.

A winning tradition helps.

Christensen, an inventive offensive coordinator whose spread attack helped Missouri get into the national spotlight and the Big 12 championship game, was contacted about a number of different head coaching opportunities before choosing Wyoming. When researching each opening, Christensen would always uncover a reason not to take the job.

"I tried to find reasons why you couldn't win at Wyoming," Christensen said. "Those weren't coming up."

So Christensen accepted the challenge of becoming the latest coach to attempt to restore the glory to Cowboy football.

He has the support of UW president Tom Buchanan and athletics director Tom Burman. He has state of the art facilities, including the Rochelle Athletic Center, a behemoth indoor practice facility and a refurbished War Memorial Stadium. And he has a loyal fan base, at least for now, that is dying for something to stand up and cheer about.

"I didn't want to go to a place where football wasn't important to the community and the state. I didn't want to coach in an empty stadium," Christensen said. "I think Wyoming, on a smaller level, is similar to

Nebraska. People drive from all over the state to support the football program . . . . The people of Wyoming are so passionate, even more than I imagined. Traveling to different cities and towns across the state, the warm welcome we've received and the excitement about the program has been pretty neat."

There are still recruiting hurdles for the head coach at Wyoming to clear.

"What I found in my first year is the biggest hurdle is not getting kids to commit to Wyoming. The real challenge is getting them to visit," Christensen said. "Once they visit, it's an easy sell. I believe 85 percent of the kids we had visit committed. We went with an approach that we were going to throw out a lot bigger net. We signed kids from 13 different states. If we get a lead on a kid and there's an interest of some sort, we're willing to go anywhere."

In 2008, Utah, also a member of the Mountain West Conference, finished second in the polls with a perfect 13-0 record, including a 31-17 victory over Alabama in the Sugar Bowl. The Utes defeated Wyoming 40-7 at War Memorial Stadium, but Christensen believes the gap can be closed.

"We've got a little ways to go. The encouraging thing was I didn't feel as far behind from a talent standpoint as I did when we got to Missouri in the Big 12," Christensen said. "We're going to have to have some good recruiting years and win bowls and get players excited to come here. But we're not real far behind and right now we're just focusing on the day by day process."

For over four decades many Cowboy fans have been wondering if the program will ever be on college football's biggest stage again. Christensen said he defines success at Wyoming as producing winning seasons in the competitive Mountain West Conference and appearing in minor bowls (Las Vegas Bowl, New Mexico Bowl and Poinsettia Bowl) on a consistent basis.

But if the stars and schedule should align just right . . . .

"Utah showed that if you do the right things and build the program the right way and build a consistent winner you're going to have an opportunity for something special," Christensen said.

The 14 black players on the 1969 UW football team were by far the largest contingent at that point in the program's history. But they were by no means the first to take the football field for the Cowboys. A 1931 brochure in the UW Athletic Department archives shows two African-Americans on that team. One of them was Taft Harris from Casper, whose name appears on the Natrona County High School's hall of fame for winning numerous letters. Harris also played on the UW basketball team in the early 30s.

The photographs in that 1931 publication indicate that a player identified as P. Parkhurst may also have been an African-American. No other publications from the 30s were found in the archives, but programs from 1946-60 indicate that no African-Americans played on those teams. Very few appear among the photos of the opposing teams either. One of them was James Jordan, a halfback on the Denver Pioneers when they played at Memorial Stadium in 1949. (19)

In 1960, Curt Jimerson and Ron Bostick were believed to be the first blacks to play basketball at Wyoming. But the photographic evidence shows Harris was the original pioneer. Jimerson had a great career with the Cowboys under Bill Strannigan and eventually became one of the first black FBI agents. Bostick only stayed on the team for one season.

At the 100th anniversary celebration of Cowboy basketball, legends Charles Bradley, Fennis Dembo, Flynn Robinson and Reginald Slater paid tribute to Jimerson for paving the way for their brilliant collegiate careers.

"They all came up and personally thanked me for opening the door," said Jimerson, who averaged 17.5 points per game as a senior in 1961-62. "That meant a lot to me." (20)

The first African-American football player at Wyoming in the post-World War II era appears to be Mike Walker, a sophomore halfback from Detroit, who was photographed in the UW 1961 football game program. Walker is not there the next year, but Alan Johnson and Dave Marion, both running backs from Bakersfield, California are shown.

In 1963, Earland Ezell, a tailback from Grand Rapids, Michigan, appears in the programs. Beginning in 1964 and most likely continuing each year until the present day, the Cowboys' rosters have included at least two African-Americans.

Besides the three members of the Black 14 who returned to the team in 1970, the roster that year included three new African-Americans and by 1972 that number was up to nine. (19)

The Right Man at the Wrong Time

Wyoming's football history includes a long list of accomplished head coaches—names like Bowden Wyatt, Phil Dickens, Bob Devaney, Paul Roach and Joe Tiller.

Leonard Frank Shurmur may have had the brightest football mind of them all.

Unfortunately, the beloved "Fritz" was named the Cowboys head coach during the program's darkest era.

The nationally ranked Cowboys crumbled after the Black 14 incident. Lloyd Eaton's record was 54-20-2 before it happened and 3-13-0 in the sad aftermath.

After Eaton coached his final game in 1970, completing a miserable 1-9 season, athletic director Glenn "Red" Jacoby turned to the brilliant defensive coach to put the pieces back together.

Shurmur managed to post a 5-6 campaign in 1971, his first season as head coach, but that was as good as it would get on the scoreboard for the Pokes. He compiled a 15-29 record in four seasons before getting fired after a 2-9 finish in 1974.

"Fritz was a very good person. He did the best job he could do under the circumstances," said Gene Huey, a longtime NFL assistant who was given his first coaching opportunity by Shurmur on his UW staff. "The situation didn't help Wyoming's fortunes in football. They struggled to get athletes."

As an assistant before the Black 14 incident, Shurmur was able to help lure some of the best talent in the country to Laramie and turned promising players into All-Americans and NFL draft picks.

The most intriguing and potentially dominant player Fritz recruited and coached at UW was Tony McGee. In the end, they had a lot in common—both were defensive gems from Michigan, both were good enough to win Super Bowls, and both were asked to leave the Wyoming football program.

"Tony was 6-4, 240 pounds and he was also the fastest guy on our team," said John Griffin, a member of the Black 14 who later became a graduate assistant under Shurmur. "He was faster than me or Ivie Moore or Joe Williams or Ted Williams. He was a rare guy who can do it all, like a Lawrence Taylor back in the day or a Deacon Jones. When he came off that end there was no way to stop him."

Even today, elite defensive linemen are tough to find in the NFL, let alone at the college ranks. As any defensive coordinator worth his salt will tell you: it all starts up front.

And in 1967, Wyoming landed a defensive lineman for the ages when McGee decided to play in Laramie instead of at Michigan State or Nebraska.

The Battle Creek, Michigan, native went to the same church as Dick Speights, a standout defensive back for the Cowboys from 1965-67. That certainly helped Eaton's staff during the recruiting process.

But it was a personal visit to McGee's home from Shurmur—who had grown up in Wyandotte, Michigan, a suburb south of Detroit where his father did his best to grind out a better life for his family as a factory worker for 49 years—that ultimately sealed the deal.

"I had a full scholarship to Michigan State and turned that down when they were co-national champions with Notre Dame (1966). Then I signed with Nebraska and changed my mind on that," McGee said. "Fritz Shurmur did a good job coming to my house. He realized I was a good player and knew it more than even I did."

McGee's high school team, Battle Creek Central, was 33-0 in games that he played in and won a state championship. And McGee wasn't expecting to lose much at Wyoming either, after joining a program coming off back-to-back 10-1 seasons and an appearance in the Sugar Bowl.

As a freshman, however, there was an adjustment to chasing quarterbacks at 7,220 feet.

"It was different because I had never played in that kind of altitude. I couldn't breathe," McGee said. "I played both ways as a tight end and defensive end on the freshmen team. I was excited, my first scrimmage I caught two touchdowns and showed the coaches that I was a good pass rusher."

During the 1968 season, McGee was a situational pass rusher playing behind senior Frank Pescatore. The Cowboys earned a share of a third consecutive WAC championship that season with a 7-3 record but opened the campaign with a tough 13-10 loss at Nebraska and closed it with a hard-to-swallow 14-7 loss at Arizona.

"Losing our last game cost us a bowl," McGee said. "It was a very emotional game and I remember I had an interception. We knew if we won that game we would have gone to a bowl and it was tough."

Wyoming's next game, the 1969 season-opener at War Memorial Stadium, was a rematch against Arizona. Shurmur's defense exacted some sweet revenge with a 23-7 victory.

The other loss in '68 was a 10-3 defensive struggle at Air Force. The Cowboys had to make the trip to the Academy again in '69, but escaped with a 27-25 win this time.

McGee finished that game with seven sacks and had 11 quarterback takedowns through the first four games of the 1969 season. He was drooling at the thought of wreaking some havoc in the BYU backfield the following Saturday.

"I had a great deal riding on that season and I was having a very good year," McGee said.

Anthony Eugene McGee would never play another down for Wyoming. The Black 14 incident changed his path to the top of the football mountain and sent the Cowboys reeling into the 1970s under Shurmur.

Shurmur turned out to be a great football coach, but as a kid his best sport was baseball. In fact, Fritz was a promising major league prospect as a teenager.

"The St. Louis Cardinals wanted to sign him to a minor league contract for more money than he could understand at that time," Fritz's oldest daughter Sally Ann Shurmur said. "He met my mom in math class as a sophomore in high school. They talked about him going to play professionally, but it was old-school travel by bus and playing however many days in a row and being away from home. So they agreed mutually that that wasn't what they wanted to do."

Fritz received a small stipend to play baseball and football at Albion (Michigan) College, where he was a Little All-American on the gridiron, but not on the defensive side of the ball. He was a center. And memorizing what the 11 guys on the other side of the line of scrimmage were supposed to do to stop him or get his quarterback helped mold Shurmur into a great coach. He began his coaching career as a graduate assistant at Albion while pursing his Master's degree.

"His players were a big part of our life and they were always over at the house," Sally Ann said. "I was born in the middle of July and my first outing was to football practice in a big buggy. It was a beautiful day and my dad threw a real football in my buggy. That's not made up. And people to this day think it's really odd that as a woman I'm the biggest football fan they know."

The Shurmurs' lives would change forever when Fritz received a call from Eaton, who cut his coaching teeth at Alma (Michigan) College, to join him at Wyoming in 1962.

The family was all on board to seize the opportunity, but Fritz had to board the first train he could catch out of Detroit to Laramie by himself to get a head start on the season. The close-knit family would call Wyoming home for the next 12 years.

"It was all about family growing up," Sally Ann said. "The entire time we were in Wyoming, the only vacations we took were to see relatives. We never went to Disneyland; our vacations were always going back to Michigan. And my dad could also combine them with recruiting trips."

To steal local talent like McGee.

Had McGee gone to Michigan State, he wouldn't have been overly friendly with his peers who were playing at Michigan. Had he gone to Nebraska, he wouldn't have had a lot of warm feelings for Oklahoma players. But there would have been mutual respect after the rivalry games were over.

Four decades later, McGee still insists that the BYU players crossed the line against the Cowboys and that the planned protest of the 1969 game by the Black 14 was justified.

"I want to make it clear that it was nothing against Wyoming. The whole thing was against Brigham Young," McGee said. "They had called us names and taken cheap shots for years while the officials acted like they did not see it. And they told us we couldn't worship in their church as equals."

McGee said the lack of public support from the coaches over the way the black players felt they were being mistreated by their BYU counterparts was disappointing.

And then insult was added to the injured feelings in 1969 when Eaton took the Black 14 into the Fieldhouse on that fateful Friday and told the players that they were the ones who had betrayed him with their plan to protest the Mormon Church.

Eaton, who was clearly upset that the players had challenged his authority, told them that as far as he was concerned, they could go back to their "colored relief" and play at traditional black colleges like Grambling or Morgan State.

"Just to be sure we knew what he meant by colored relief he said, 'negro relief,'" McGee said. "As if all colored people needed relief."

McGee left Laramie after the incident to resume his career and education at Bishop College, a small all-black Baptist school in Texas that opened in 1881 and closed in 1988. The NFL scouts were still able to find him, but he says the stigma over what happened at Wyoming followed him throughout his storied career.

In the 1971 draft, the Chicago Bears selected McGee in the third round. He believes he would have been a first-round pick if not for the Black 14 incident.

"When I was drafted, someone in personnel with the Los Angeles Rams told me I was going to be the Rams' first-round pick but the coaches and people at Wyoming said I was the main instigator (of the Black 14)," McGee said. "I wasn't, but they still soured on me."

McGee went on to have a brilliant 14-year NFL career that included winning a Super Bowl with the Washington Redskins. He thought about his black teammates at Wyoming throughout the journey.

"When you reflect back on the whole thing, we thought we were doing it for the right reasons," McGee said. "It was nothing against coach Eaton or the staff or the university or the state . . . .

"Everyone made us the villains, but you have to think about the statement about colored relief."

Most of the Black 14 were focused on Eaton during his rant in the Fieldhouse. For some reason, Tony Gibson was drawn to Fritz.

"I remember looking at his face and when Eaton said those words, his mouth just dropped open and he shook his head," Gibson said. "It's something I'll never forget. And of course back in those days, as a loyal assistant, he's not going to say anything to go against the head coach."

Not in public at least.

Shurmur and Paul Roach did try to talk Eaton into reconsidering his decision to kick the 14 players off the team, meeting with him in his office with the door shut. But Eaton made that a short, one-sided meeting as well.

"He was devastated that those kids who had been given the opportunity of a lifetime, to be given an education, would go against the wishes of their head coach," Sally Ann said of her dad's initial reaction to the Black 14 incident. "That was the first time I was aware that any players of his really defied authority.

"Looking back on it, when you think about it 40 years later and you recall personal recollections and conversations, it's heart-wrenching because upon his death the people who knew him the best said the uniqueness of Fritz Shurmur is he was always a team guy. It was never about him."

And then, suddenly, it was about head coach Fritz Shurmur. At least that's the way most of the spoiled fans and media saw it as the program struggled to recover.

After the 1970 season when Eaton stepped down as coach, he took a position in the UW Athletics Department as an assistant athletic director briefly and then became a scout with the Green Bay Packers. Roach departed following the 1969 season to become an assistant at Wisconsin before a distinguished career as an NFL assistant. After being promoted, Shurmur rolled up his sleeves and did his best to save Cowboy football.

"The Black 14 incident hampered the program for about 10 years. It killed it," said Griffin, one of the three black players who played for UW again after being kicked off the squad by Eaton. "We couldn't get the really good football players anymore. The African-American kids did not want to go there."

During Eaton's glory days, War Memorial Stadium was packed with overflow crowds of 18,000. Adding to the pressure Shurmur was already under was the bad timing of a stadium expansion with a new upper deck on the west side increasing the capacity to 25,500. Losing is painful enough. Doing it in front of thousands of empty seats makes it even tougher to swallow.

"As a freshman sitting in the students section it was much harder on me than on my dad," Sally Ann said. "He never wavered in his belief and approach. He thought they were going to get things done . . . .

"We had our chance at the big time and a taste of the big time and we couldn't take advantage of that."

Shurmur would have stayed at Wyoming for the rest of his career if given the time necessary to turn the program around, but he was let go four years into one of the toughest rebuilding projects in the country. There were signs that Wyoming had the right man in place— including a stunning 45-43 victory over No. 11 Arizona State on September 30, 1972, that stirred up the echoes at War Memorial Stadium.

"They out-coached us," Sun Devils head coach Frank Kush, whose juggernaut had won 30 of its previous 31 games, said after the wild game. "The Wyoming coaches did a great job in preparing for us." (21)

Outside the victorious locker room, Shurmur said: "It was an amazing game. In my 38 years . . . I don't think I've seen anything to rival it."

The momentum from the milestone win did not last long. In 1975, Fred Akers was hired to begin a new era of Cowboy football. A series of bright, young coaches began using Wyoming as a stepping stone job again.

"The thing I felt best about was that we were not going to compromise the integrity of the university or the program," the classy Fritz said. "We knew (the program) would come back and that nobody had to cheat. We ran out of time, which is part of the business. We made some strides, but we stalled at the end. The University of Wyoming was awfully good to me." (21)

In 1976, coaching Shurmur's recruits, Akers guided the Cowboys to an 8-3 record in the regular season and an appearance in the Fiesta Bowl. He would leave for Texas after the season and focused more on recruiting for the Longhorns than preparing for Oklahoma. UW was drubbed 41-7 in a Fiesta Bowl the Laramie Boomerang's Steve Luhn described as a "fiasco bowl."

The program went through four more head coaches before Roach returned two decades after the Black 14 incident to finish Fritz's quest of restoring some honor and glory to Wyoming football.

Shurmur went on to become one of the most respected defensive coordinators in NFL history. During one of his many successful stops around the league he crossed paths with McGee again with the New England Patriots.

Almost 10 years after the Black 14 separated the genius teacher and the gifted student, they were working together on a daily basis. One day after practice on the way to their cars, the two stopped and started talking about the past. The conversation in the parking lot went on for hours.

"We understood that both sides could have handled it a lot differently," McGee said. "I harbor no hard feelings. It was a time in life when those things were supposed to transpire. It changed a lot of lives and it didn't turn out great for everyone, but it had to be done. And it was an eye-opener."

As McGee's career was winding down in Washington, he received a phone call from a loyal Cowboy fan who wanted to let him know how he felt about the Black 14.

"It was a guy from Wyoming who said, 'They didn't treat you right, give me a call if you ever need anything,'" McGee said. "That gentleman was Senator Al Simpson. We still talk periodically. I always thought that was very nice of him and it was unsolicited."

Simpson, a former defensive lineman at UW in the early 1950s, had watched McGee's spectacular play from the stands at War Memorial Stadium through his binoculars.

"When I played for Bowden Wyatt, my job was to rear up under the center and hit him under the chin until he got tired of centering the ball," Simpson said. "Nothing fancy, but I was pretty good. So I just liked watching guys like Tony McGee and Larry Nels. I can see them moving in my mind's eye right now . . . .

"When I got out to Washington (as a U.S. Senator) I called Tony and told him I'd love to have lunch with him. We still see each other once in awhile. The beautiful part about Tony, like Nelson Mandela when he got out of the prison at Robben Island, is he never had any bitterness."

Thirty years after Wyoming's Sugar Bowl appearance, Shurmur returned to New Orleans to coach in another important game—Super Bowl XXXI.

With Mike Holmgren and Brett Favre in control of the offense and Shurmur coordinating the Reggie White-led defense, the Green Bay Packers finally brought the Lombardi Trophy back home to "Title Town" with a victory over Bill Parcells' Patriots at the Super-dome.

Fritz's amazing but sometimes difficult career had come full circle in the Big Easy.

"After the coaches had endured media day that week we had about a two-minute chat on the phone and I've never heard my dad that excited during my life," Sally Ann said. "It was abundantly clear that we had to win this game . . . . Thirty years earlier I thought winning the Sugar Bowl would have been a big bonus. Nobody remembers who lost the Super Bowl. To get to the pinnacle, it was definitely his shining moment. There's no doubt about that."

Shurmur, who spent 24 seasons coaching in the NFL, was asked if it bothered him that he had never been a head coach in the league.

"At one time," he said, "I was too young and then I was too old. I wonder what happened to the just-right years." (22)

The Black 14 happened. But Shurmur didn't use it as an excuse and never stopped working, even after winning a Super Bowl in his late 60s.

"At that point in his career he was an old man. There are not many assistants that age who want to keep working," Sally Ann said. "It's hard for an old man; they work seven days a week seven months a year and a lot of days for 15 hours. Physically, it takes its toll after a while. That's really the saddest part about how the whole thing ended."

Shurmur, forever loyal to the head coach, promised Holmgren he would go with him to Seattle in 1999 to help him make the transition from Green Bay. Fritz promised his better half, Peggy, that he would retire after two more seasons. He died at his home in Suamico, Wisconsin, of cancer before ever coaching a game with the Seahawks.

Leonard Frank Shurmur will always be remembered fondly in Green Bay. And Fritz's contributions to the Cowboys—as a young assistant in the best of times and as the head coach under the toughest of circumstances—shouldn't be forgotten in Wyoming.

"Built to Deal with Adversity"

Earl Lee was one of the best prep football players in the state of Tennessee in 1963, but the beloved Volunteers didn't recruit black players (the first African-American to suit up for the Volunteers was Lester McClain in 1968).

One of Lloyd Eaton's assistants at Wyoming, Bill Baker, was also from Tennessee and recruited Lee when he was dominating the line of scrimmage at Chattanooga's all-black Howard High School.

Baker, who was white, stuck out like a sore thumb when visiting Lee's neck of the Tennessee woods.

"We stayed on our side of the town, whites stayed on their side of the town. We were taught at a very early age how to treat white people," Lee said. "As we began to get older, things began to change and protests were taking place, even kids in the South were getting involved. It was a turbulent time of change.

"We experienced racism, but it was something that we didn't talk about or discuss very much because it was never put in our face that often."

Lee's father worked at the local steel mill and his mom was a homemaker. Both parents had a lot of questions that needed to be answered when their son told them he was going to college in Wyoming on a football scholarship.

"They really didn't know what to think. Like most black parents at the time, they were afraid of me being that far away from home without their protection," Lee said. "But I was a restless kid."

Lee made a visit to Laramie that he will never forget. Believe it or not, the climate on the high plains in the spring helped sell the prospect from Chattanooga.

"I was overwhelmed by seeing snow that late in the season. I thought it was so beautiful and clean out there. I fell in love," Lee said. "Money was a big issue for my parents, they didn't understand scholarships and they had all of the questions a poor family would have. I was the first one from my family to attend college."

Lee arrived in 1964 and played on the freshman team. He dropped out of school after the first semester and went home to work in the steel mill because all of his friends were making good money.

Soon after leaving UW, Lee was drafted and sent to Vietnam. When the military realized that his brother was already fighting in that war, they reassigned Lee to Japan and South Korea. While serving the country, Lee wrote letters to the Wyoming coaching staff to see if they would take him back into the program when his tours were completed. Eaton welcomed him back to Laramie in 1968.

"When I got back, the team had developed into a veteran team. All the guys knew each other and knew the system and the team was close-knit," Lee said.

In 1969, during the Black 14 incident, Lee said Eaton, a World War II veteran, expressed disappointment in him.

"I recall vividly the meeting with coach Eaton. He accused me of being a rabble rouser because I was older and had been in the military," Lee said. "He accused me of being the one who started all this and said I was the one who instigated it. But it was nothing like that."

After getting kicked off the team, Lee decided he would stick around and at least finish his academic career at Wyoming. He went on to become a teacher, coach and principal in the Baltimore area. The Black 14 experience was one he used throughout his career in education.

"When my kids had some problems, it taught me to take a step back and listen to the individuals I was in charge of," Lee said. "Eaton's style of leadership was OK during his generation, but it could not possibly survive today."

Lee has not returned to Laramie in four decades but would like to bring his wife to Wyoming so she can see where this story took place.

Tony Gibson had some news for the Wyoming coaches after informing them that he would indeed be coming to Laramie ready to compete for a starting position in the fall of 1969 as a fullback or running back.

"I also told them I was going to be married that summer and I was coming back with a white woman with me," Gibson says with a chuckle 40 years later. "We never gave it a thought to explain that. It didn't define us then and it doesn't now. Even with our daughter, it's not even an issue we need to discus."

Gibson would only spend two months in the UW football program before getting kicked to the curb with the rest of the Black 14. His marriage to his better half, Barbara, turned out to be much more stable. The couple celebrated their 40th anniversary during the summer of 2009.

Tony grew up in Pittsfield, Massachusetts, a quiet town where the Gibson's returned after college and where they still live today.

Unlike some of his Wyoming teammates who came from the south, including his longtime friend Earl Lee, Tony wasn't exposed to segregation or racial slurs growing up, even though his father was African-American and his mother was Italian.

"I wasn't aware of it until I was a little older," Tony said. "I wasn't subject to much racism here."

After high school, Gibson went all the way out to California to play football at Taft Junior College. His skills caught the eye of the Wyoming staff, and offensive assistant Paul Roach brought him to campus for a visit to see if he was interested in trying to become the next Jim Kiick.

"I was 19 years old, in good shape and ready to go," Gibson said. "As we were playing the first couple games, we could tell that we had a great team. I believe we had the No. 1 defense in the country. We had an excellent program."

The athletic department even helped Barbara, who had worked in the student activities office at Boston University before joining her new husband in Laramie, secure a similar position at UW. She had experienced student demonstrations on other college campuses.

"Student activism was no big deal to me. When you think of the 60s, student activism was a part of college life," Barbara said. "So when you talk about BYU and Mormons and the fact that the players were going to wear black armbands, it was no big deal to me. And I didn't think it was going to be a big deal for Wyoming."

Even though some of the other players had told Tony he didn't have to participate because he was married and had more to lose, he didn't hesitate to be a part of the plan to protest and had no idea it would become a national story.

"I don't think anybody gave it a thought. We were just going to walk in there and talk to the coach," Tony said. "I remember him taking us to the upper bleachers inside the Fieldhouse and we all sat down there. Joe Williams started to ask him a question and he didn't get four words out of his mouth and that's when Eaton started to lambaste us.

"We were just dumbfounded. I never thought in a million years something like that was going to happen."

Lionel "Dowdy" Grimes was an all-state football player in high school, which was an impressive accolade considering he grew up in Alliance, Ohio, a football-crazed town in the northeastern part of the football-crazed Buckeye State.

"It was football country," Grimes said. "We used to say that within that 100-mile radius in Ohio and western Pennsylvania was where the best football players in the country came from. When I went to Wyoming, I tried to tell that to the players from Texas and California."

What Grimes didn't tell the coaches at Wyoming during his brief collegiate football career was that his true love was baseball. After being dismissed from the UW team by Lloyd Eaton in 1969, Grimes was able to pursue his true passion. But not before the military attempted to send him to Vietnam.

"I got my draft notice right after I got kicked out," Grimes said. "I don't know if they sent our names out or what. But I didn't pass the physical because I had a knee injury from playing football."

Eventually, Grimes enrolled at Findlay College (now Findlay University) back in his native Ohio and found it to be the perfect fit for his educational needs and athletic skills. He graduated with a B.S. in marketing after playing three seasons on the baseball team.

"The athletic program was always fair and consistent," said Grimes, who also has a lot of praise for Dr. James Houdeshell's role as athletic director and coach during his Findlay days. (23)

Grimes, a student body president in high school and the football team's captain, said he had never really experienced any political or racial tensions while studying and playing alongside white kids in Ohio.

"Growing up, athletics was always the closest thing to being fair," Grimes said. "And after the Black 14, that wasn't the case anymore."

Grimes took a bus from Laramie to Denver after the Black 14 incident. Still a teenager, he was a little lost. And so was his luggage.

After graduating from Findlay, Grimes went to work for the Ford Motor Co. in the marketing department for 16 years. Later, he had his own car dealership in Delaware, Ohio. Grimes is now a semi-retired consultant living in Columbus.

With plenty of encouragement from "Dowdy," seven other members of the Grimes family have gone to school at Findlay, including his son, Jaison, who was a pre-med graduate before attending medical school at Ohio State to become a neurologist.

Grimes returned to Laramie in 1993 for the 100th anniversary of Cowboy football. It was difficult to avoid thinking about what might have been during that trip.

"Out of the 14 of us, there would have been about 10 or 11 that could have gone into the NFL," Grimes said. "We were a very strong team, no doubt about it. The WAC would have been ours again for sure . . . .

"I'm not surprised that most of us went on to be successful after the Black 14. We were all good athletes but we also had strong character. We were built to deal with that adversity."

Cowboys Once Again

Forty years later, Don Meadows describes those directly involved in the Black 14 incident—including Lloyd Eaton, the coaching staff, the white players and the black players—this way: "We're all nice people. Both sides made mistakes."

The forgiving Meadows heard some hurtful words from each side of the conflict. He was called a "nigger" and threatened by anonymous cowards over the phone after being kicked off the team in 1969. He was also labeled an "Uncle Tom" by some of his black peers after returning to the program and playing for Eaton again in 1970 along with John Griffin and Ted Williams.

"I got close to a lot of really nice people," Meadows reflected. "If you discount the ugly parts of '69 and the '70 football season, I have nothing but fond memories of Wyoming. I experienced a lot of good things. I guess I made the best of a bad situation."

Meadows spent his early childhood in Houston until the family moved to Denver when he was 11. He had a stellar career at Manual High School, and like most Colorado kids he wanted to play for the Buffaloes in Boulder.

CU had recruited Meadows during his dominant prep career, but his grades weren't quite up to par to get into the university. So he began his collegiate career at Mesa College (now called Mesa State) in Grand Junction. When he was ready to transfer to a major program, he had a change of heart and opted for Wyoming, which was coming off three consecutive WAC championships, instead of CU, which had closed the 1968 season with four consecutive losses and a 4-6 record.

"I wanted to be a nose guard and got my shot at Wyoming," Meadows said. "At the beginning of that first season (in 1969), I was having a good time, everybody was. We always sat around the locker room after practice and were enjoying it."

Meadows said that when he was playing at Mesa College, a junior-college powerhouse, which at the time fed star players to prominent programs, it was understood that the head coach would not play a black player if he found out that player was dating a white girl.

Unlike in Laramie, where Meadows hadn't gotten to know his coaches or teammates very well before the dismissal, Meadows felt comfortable enough with his standing in the locker room to challenge the Mesa coach on the racist policy.

"I confronted the coach in a meeting with all of the white players," Meadows said. "And he backed down and changed his thoughts and left it alone."

Meadows said when the Black 14 held its initial meeting about wearing the armbands, he wanted to get the white Cowboys on board before taking the issue to Eaton.

"I suggested that we talk to the white players and everybody shouted me down," Meadows said. "So they kind of distanced themselves from me."

Meadows had not played against BYU before. The black players who had done so say they experienced racial taunts and cheap shots during their encounters with the Cougars, which fueled their investigation into the LDS policies and their desire to protest.

But in Meadows' view, the influence of Willie Black, the chancellor of the Black Student Alliance on campus, and William Waterman, the NAACP attorney who investigated Eaton's decision to kick the 14 black players off the team and represented the group in court, exacerbated the situation.

"For the most part Willie Black misled us. At least I felt that way, like he didn't let us know the full ramifications of what was happening," Meadows said. "There was peer pressure. And some of the lesser known players became militant overnight . . . . They all started believing what Willie Black was having to say, and I was still pretty distant."

Meadows said he practiced at a very high level early in the week and was really looking forward to the game against BYU. After the Black 14 incident, he was holding out hope that UW president William Carlson and the board of trustees would overturn Eaton's decision and reinstate the players.

"I wasn't political," Meadows said. "I didn't know what was going on. I was hurt because I came there to play football. It shook me up when we were dismissed from the team."

John Griffin was a great route runner back in the day and has the ability to sum up October 17, 1969, just as precisely.

"It was a snapshot in time," Griffin said. "It was a moment that ruined (Lloyd) Eaton's career and the Wyoming program."

For a cool kid from southern California who grew up with a surfboard and awash in diversity, being told by the head football coach that he could go back to the Morgan States and Grambling States of the college world was a stunningly ignorant point of view.

Griffin's grandma lived in Hollywood. His father was a very successful accountant in the Los Angeles area. And if he were forced to "go back" somewhere, well, he spent his childhood hanging around the pristine and diverse UCLA campus.

"It was a melting pot," Griffin said of San Fernando, California, his hometown. "Whites, blacks, Asians, Hispanics, we had a little bit of everything. And we all got along. I can't remember one time in San Fernando Junior High or San Fernando High School experiencing racial problems."

Jim Mora, who later became an NFL head coach with the Indianapolis Colts and New Orleans Saints, was Griffin's football coach in junior high. His high school team was loaded with talent and determined to win the L.A. city title in 1966.

"I went back there in about 1993 and visited one of our coaches, Howard Marcus, and he said he had something to show me and he had every picture of all of us from that '66 team on the wall," Griffin reminisced. "We had an incredible football team. It was a commitment the 22 players made along with our coaches that we were going to focus and be the best in L.A. Everyone cut their hair before the season, we reported in shape and we even had brand new uniforms."

San Fernando made it to the championship game but lost to Carson High at East L.A. City College Stadium.

Griffin had the grades to get into any four-year university on his list but chose to continue the pursuit of his professional football dreams at Pierce College in Woodland Hills, California. He grew from a 5-8, 156-pound high school senior into a 5-10, 166-pound split end / strong safety with major college skills.

Upon visiting Laramie, Griffin, who rode horses at his grandparents' farm in Texas as a child, was sold on Wyoming and the challenge of trying to become the next Gene Huey.

"My dad asked, 'Why are you going to Wyoming?'" said Griffin, who had other offers to stay in California. "But I've always been a city boy who loved the country. I also knew about what the program had accomplished and that this was a pretty good breeding ground for professional athletes."

Griffin arrived on campus in the summer of 1969 and took a job laying sod. He practiced and bonded with his new teammates in the evenings as they prepared for what they believed was going to be an 11-0 season.

Everything was perfect as the Cowboys opened the season with victories over Arizona, Air Force, Colorado State and Texas-El Paso. Griffin and his roommate, Ron Hill, were part of a deep and dangerous receiving unit for quarterback Ed Synakowski (to throw to).

"That's why it was so tragic what happened to us. Had that team remained intact, we not only would have won the WAC in '66, '67 and '68, it would have been the same in '69, '70 and '71," Griffin said. "There was nothing stopping us, and being as good as we were, we could have attracted even better athletes."

Griffin remembers officials from the Sugar Bowl scouting Wyoming early in the '69 season, prior to the

Black 14 incident, to consider extending another invitation to the program should it run the table in the regular season again.

"We could have gone to the Sugar Bowl and won it this time," Griffin said.

The Cowboys beat the Cougars and then San Jose State to climb to a 6-0 record and No. 13 ranking before the attrition caught up to the coach on the scoreboard. Wyoming lost its final four games in 1969 and finished the 1970 season 1-9.

Griffin was one of three members of the Black 14 to return to the program and suffer through Eaton's last season with him.

In order to be reinstated, Griffin had to take 19 ½ credit hours to get caught up academically while working nights at the library and of course getting the coach's permission to play again.

"I was in Laramie the whole time. I had to mull it over. My parents let me make my decision," Griffin said. "I only had one year of eligibility left, so if I would have left my football career would have been over. Don (Meadows) suggested that I petition to get back on the team . . . . I went right to Eaton and thought he would be a real ass about it, but he was not condescending at all. He said the other players would have to make the decision."

The players welcomed Griffin back, but the losing coupled with the Black 14 incident dashed his dream of playing in the NFL. Eaton, an excellent evaluator of talent at Wyoming and later as a scout for the Green Bay Packers, knew his talented split end should have been drafted.

"I just accepted that it was over until Eaton that spring called me into his office and said, 'I know you can play and I'm going to try to help you,'" Griffin said. "He made some calls to the Canadian Football League (CFL), and the Winnipeg Blue Bombers sent me a $13,000 contract."

Griffin headed north of the border, but only briefly, before deciding to put his UW degree to use during a rewarding career for the YMCA and later in the corporate world.

"In the summer of '71, I went to Winnipeg and was going to make the team, but I lost interest in playing football," Griffin said. "It hit me like a brick that this was no longer fun for me."

Griffin, who is retired and living in Denver, returned to Laramie with the Columbine High School football team recently to help the young players during a camp at UW. Then head coach Joe Glenn called Paul Roach to tell him that there was an old but familiar face on the practice field, and soon the two old friends were reunited.

"I don't regret it," Griffin said of his decision to attend Wyoming. "Even though the Black 14 thing happened . . . certain things build character over the years and that's essentially what it did for me."

The Man in the Mirror

So how did you end up becoming the Wyoming athletic director?

When asked the question decades later during an interview for this book, Paul Roach begins to laugh, and laugh, and laugh . . . funny story.

Roach had returned to Laramie to help the athletic department get back on the winning track by serving as the director of the Cowboy Joe Club. He put 18,000 miles on his Buick, memorizing every inch of the state's highways while raising money one hand shake or Sugar Bowl story at a time.

About 10 months into the gifting gig, athletic director Gary Cunningham, who had played basketball for John Wooden at UCLA, left Wyoming to accept the same position at Fresno State. The Board of Trustees summoned Roach to see if he was interested in a promotion.

"They called me downstairs and asked me if I'd like to be the athletic director. So I took the job," Roach said. "Then another funny thing happened, about six months later (UW head coach) Dennis Erickson took the job at Washington State."

Erickson was the nomad who would leave Washington State for Miami en route to Seattle (Seahawks), Oregon State, San Francisco (49ers), Idaho and Arizona State. When Erickson left Laramie after one season, posting a 6-6 record with the Pokes in 1986, all of the Cowboy Joe supporters whom Roach had won over were not amused.

Erickson didn't even bother to return to Laramie to clean out his office.

"I got a hold of him on the phone and I said, 'Dennis, aren't you going to come back and get your family?'" Roach said. "He said, 'Don't worry, I'll send for them.'

"Then I asked if he'd like to say goodbye to the team. He said: 'You can do that for me.'"

Roach called a team meeting and explained what happened. He told the players to focus on their academics and that he would hire a coach worthy of them in 10 days to two weeks.

"I said, 'I'll do everything possible to get you a good one," Roach said.

He was a man of his word. Roach decided that the most qualified candidate to lead Wyoming football back to the top of the conference mountain was staring at him in the mirror.

It proved to be one of the best hires in the program's history.

"After some meetings and talking to a couple trustees and the president, I called another team meeting," Roach said. "I walked in and said, 'Well, you've got a new football coach and you're looking at him."

When Roach left UW after the 1969 season, the program was on the way down and Eaton would soon be on his way out. Shurmur did his best to save the sinking ship but struggled to recruit the black athlete as the Black 14 incident continued to be an ominous cloud hanging over the program. Then a series of talented young coaches—Fred Akers, Pat Dye and Erickson, used Wyoming as a stepping stone to bigger jobs.

In order for the Cowboys to emerge from the football abyss, the coaching staff would have to put together a special group of players capable of over-achieving.

Wyoming, once on the verge of becoming a college football powerhouse in the late '60s, would only return to the national stage as a Cinderella story.

The unlikely star of the rebirth turned out to be Randy Welniak, an unheralded recruit from Ord, Nebraska.

"Ord was definitely a small town. The population is around 2,500 and we lived out on a farm and ranch seven miles outside of town," Welniak said. "It was a great small town to grow up in, a bit sheltered looking back on it now. I was fortunate to grow up in that type of community . . . . Even though we were a small high school we played in Class B, which was the second-highest classification. And we competed at a pretty high level."

The head coach, Gene Suhr, tried to simulate what the Nebraska Cornhuskers were doing offensively under legendary coach Tom Osborne. That, of course, included running the option. But Suhr also knew Welniak was a special player and allowed him to break the huddle in a pro-type set and throw the ball 15 times a game.

Winning football games on Friday nights was an important escape for Welniak, whose father died when he was 13, leaving behind a wife and seven kids.

"We all took on additional responsibilities and continued to run the farm and ranch. We turned a very negative thing into a positive. We have a close, tight-knit family," Welniak said. "Having our football coach as a role model was instrumental. One of my brothers was a year older and it was important for him to give him direction, guidance, discipline. And we had a great work ethic growing up on a farm and ranch."

Like all high school football players in Nebraska, Welniak's dream was to play for the Huskers at fabled Memorial Stadium in Lincoln. The best Osborne could do for the undersized quarterback from Ord was offer him an opportunity to walk on.

Although tempting, there was another option: A scholarship offer from Wyoming.

Welniak, who was every bit as gifted in the classroom as he was on the gridiron, accepted the free education and played two years for Al Kincaid (1984-85), about eight months for Erickson (1986) and then waited for Roach to tell him who his third head coach in four years would be.

"When he called the meeting and said he was going to be the coach, well, Paul's a funny guy and we didn't know if he was being sarcastic or telling the truth," Welniak said. "And then he went on and explained why, told us about his background. A lot of us had no idea that he had that much coaching experience. What a blessing that was. That was the best thing to happen to Wyoming football since I've been around."

Twenty years after the Sugar Bowl season, Roach led the Cowboys to another WAC championship, an appearance in the Holiday Bowl, and a 10-3 record, including an emotional 29-27 road victory over BYU. Wyoming trailed 14-0 at halftime before scoring 29 unanswered points in the third quarter, highlighted by three Craig Burnett touchdown passes, and holding off a late Cougars drive.

"Wow, what a game we had," Roach said when reminded of the rare Pokes victory in Provo. "We were down big and came back and scored a bunch of touchdowns to win it. That was a big comeback."

But it was nothing like Welniak's comeback story. He had planned to be the one breaking the huddle during the return to glory in 1987, but during spring drills leading up to it, he sustained a serious injury to his throwing shoulder that required reconstructive surgery.

"The doctors said I would never throw again. That was heart-wrenching," Welniak said. "I thought, 'Well, maybe I can play receiver?'"

Welniak put the shoulder through an extensive rehabilitation regimen over the summer but still didn't have complete flexibility or strength in the arm when the players reported back for fall camp. So he redshirted in 1987 and quietly prepared for his one chance to finish his football career in the spotlight.

"The biggest question mark about the 1988 team, from a fan and media perspective, was the quarterback," Welniak said.

Roach, a master at getting the most out of his field generals, named Welniak as his starter without hesitation before the season kicked off on ESPN. In the opener on September 1, the first night game ever played at War Memorial Stadium, he led Wyoming to a 24-14 upset of nationally ranked and preseason WAC favorite BYU.

"It was just an unbelievable atmosphere. People were excited," Welniak said. "To dominate them like we did . . . our defense was so good. Ty Detmer's initiation occurred that night because our defense controlled the line of scrimmage."

On September 24, Wyoming's defense didn't have control of anything at Falcon Stadium. Air Force took a 21-point lead into the fourth quarter and appeared to be well on the way to handing the Cowboys their first loss of the season. And then Welniak led his offense to scores on all five of its drives in the fourth quarter, setting up Sean Fleming's 27-yard field goal in the final seconds that proved to be the difference in a 48-45 Wyoming victory.

"It really didn't sink in until after the game," said Welniak, who finished with 359 passing yards and 109 rushing yards. "We knew it was a pivotal game in the season and we got down by 28 points. But we still had a lot of confidence in our offense and knew we could score. The defense had key turnovers for us and it was just an amazing finish to get the ball back with 40 seconds left. It was an amazing game that I will remember for the rest of my life."

Wyoming would open the season 10-0 with Welniak as the starter and cracked the top 10 in the national polls. The Pokes lost at Houston on November 12 and were run over by Barry Sanders and the Oklahoma State Cowboys in the Holiday Bowl. But at 11-2, the Wyoming football team was able to sing "Ragtime Cowboy Joe," the school fight song, after more victories than any team in program history.

Players of Welniak's size don't get recruited to play quarterback very often anymore, even at Wyoming. But Roach had an accurate measure of the heart of the kid from Ord, and together they brought the magic back to Laramie.

Paul Roach's brilliant football career started with single-wing football. He played quarterback and line-backer at Rapid City (South Dakota) Central High School in the late 1940s before moving to the offensive line at Black Hills Teachers College and graduating in 1952.

His first jobs were at rural high schools and small colleges in the Dakotas. While attending a coaching clinic in Bemidji, Minnesota, Roach hit it off with another bright mind in his profession who had also played college football in Spearfish, South Dakota.

Lloyd Eaton would not forget their discussions of all things Xs and Os, and offered Roach a chance to be part of his staff at Wyoming in 1962 after taking over for Bob Devaney.

"When he contacted me, he seemed to know quite a bit more about me and my record and where I had been," Roach said. "I suppose that was part of the interview. It was exciting to join the staff at Wyoming, and we got off to a good start."

After the Black 14 incident Roach went to Wisconsin before moving on to a distinguished career in the NFL that included opportunities to work on John Madden's staff with the Oakland Raiders, as coach Bart Starr's offensive coordinator with the Green Bay Packers and as part of Red Miller's magical run with the Denver Broncos (1977-80).

"There was just something about that team," Roach said of the '77 Broncos. "The character of that team was really outstanding. A lot of that is attributed to the coach, Red Miller. And we also had a really great defensive coordinator in Joe Collier."

Denver, led by Collier's "Orange Crush" defense, defeated Oakland in the AFC Championship game and made the long suffering franchise's first appearance in the Super Bowl, a 27-10 loss to Tom Landry's Cowboys.

"When we played Dallas in the Super Bowl after the 1977 season, I can remember preparing for the game and looking at the film over and over to try and find ways to be successful," Roach said. "But Dallas had a really good team with really good defensive linemen . . . . One thing I think about, because it would have helped us, is how we only had one week between the AFC Championship and the Super Bowl. We were right under the gun and I think if we had two weeks to prepare like they do now, it would have helped us."

Roach went into private business as the 1980s began and felt like his dream of being a head coach had faded away. And then he had the chance to hire himself at Wyoming. The old Cowboy would breathe the life back into the program he loved two decades after its darkest chapter.

Roach, the only man to serve in the dual capacity of athletics director and head football coach, led the Cowboys to back-to-back WAC championships in 1987 and 1988, going undefeated in league play both seasons. He was named the conference's coach of the year after each title and was a two-time finalist for national coach of the year.

During his four seasons as the head coach, Wyoming compiled a 35-15 record with three bowl appearances. Including the three WAC championships (1966, 1967 and 1968) and two bowls he was a part of as one of Eaton's top assistants, Roach, who was still the athletic director when Joe Tiller led the Pokes to a share of the WAC title in 1993—has been on the sideline for six of the program's seven WAC championships and six of the 10 bowl appearances in the school's history.

So how much credit do you deserve for Wyoming's winning tradition?

When asked the question, Paul Roach begins to chuckle again . . . funny story.

"I think with those teams, most any coach would have been successful," Roach said. "Not many coaches would say that. But I'm 81 now. And we had some great players."

"Darn Good Athletes and Good Guys"

Forty years later it's still emotional for many of the Black 14 participants, on all sides, to talk about the incident.

John Griffin remembers his roommate, Ron Hill, getting into a fistfight with one of the white players on the team behind the Delta Delta Delta sorority.

"You could feel the tension wherever you went on campus," Griffin said.

Griffin can still picture the look on the face of George Herrick, a white player, when the friends bumped into one another a few hours after Lloyd Eaton's decision to kick the 14 black players off the team.

"We were close, like brothers, and the day that happened he came up to me in the Washakie Center and said, 'I'm so sorry,'" Griffin said. "And tears were streaming out of his eyes and down his face. He was upset. But he was the only one who came up to me."

Paul Roach would never say a bad word about anyone. But those who played for him at Wyoming when he was an assistant coach believe things would have been a lot different in 1969 if he had made the call on the Black 14 instead of Eaton.

"No, I was not shocked about his response," Roach said. "I think that Lloyd was a really outstanding coach. That was his character. He was a disciplined person and that's how he handled situations. And I suppose that when he was met with that particular situation, which turned out to be very critical, it was a tough situation for him. But that's the way he handled it."

Mel Hamilton stayed away from War Memorial Stadium for 12 years after watching his white teammates beat BYU the day after he was kicked off the team.

"It took me maybe five years before I could even watch a football game on TV," Hamilton said. "It was very hard for me because it would always take me back to that fateful day in October, 1969. My wife finally talked me into taking a bus to a game. We went to watch Wyoming play Brigham Young with Jim McMahon in a snowstorm (in 1981)."

Gene Huey, who was a senior in 1968, was focused on trying to make it in the NFL as a player in

October, 1969, but he still remembers exactly where he was when he heard the news about the Black 14.

"I was with the Minnesota Vikings and was driving to meetings that day when it was announced on the car radio that the 14 black athletes were kicked off the Wyoming football team," Huey said. "It was quite a shock . . . boom! It was a big punch in the stomach."

As a former team captain, Huey felt like he needed to return to Laramie as soon as possible to investigate the situation and see if he could help the two sides get back together. He spoke with several of the Black 14 and some of the coaches. And as a black athlete who thrived at Wyoming under Eaton's leadership, he has very mixed emotions about the sad ending to the story.

"I certainly was not there. I'm not trying to defend his actions because they were totally wrong in the way Eaton handled it as an adult and a head coach and with the ramifications that came upon the state and university due to his actions," Huey said. "But that's the way he was. He was his own man . . . .

"At the time when all that occurred there was no model for dealing with those sort of social problems as athletes and coaches on college campuses. It's unfortunate that's what happened; now Wyoming is the model for what not to do."

There will never be closure.

Lloyd Eaton died on March 14, 2007, after suffering a stroke at the age of 88. His sister, Doris Shipley, said he was suffering from the onset of Alzheimer's at the end of his life but that he enjoyed his retirement years in Idaho where he did a lot of fishing without expressing any regret over the Black 14 incident and the abrupt end to his once brilliant coaching career.

"I suspect everything fell apart for him for a bit," says Shipley, who is in her 90s, on the aftermath of Eaton's decision on October 17, 1969. "I think Wyoming really backed him but he was so unhappy that he had a team that did not do what he told them to do that it was time to quit if he didn't have control of his team."

Shipley believes her brother was just adhering to the principles of discipline he demanded as a coach, but she admits Eaton was a stubborn person.

"He could probably throw as good a fit or temper tantrum as anybody," Shipley said. "But they brought that on themselves because when you are told to follow a rule you should do it."

Eaton did not return to Laramie when his 1967 Sugar Bowl team was inducted into the UW Athletics Hall of Fame. He refused numerous interview requests from members of the media over the years but did reiterate his position on the Black 14 incident in the Denver Post on May 9, 1982.

When asked if he still believed in his standing rule that players could not protest or demonstrate in any way he said, "Hell yes. Demonstrations have no place in athletics, not while you're on scholarship."

Asked if he ever regretted what happened at Wyoming in 1969, he said, "Hell no. Not once."

Asked what he would say if he were to see one of the Black 14 on the street, he said, "I probably wouldn't recognize him. He'd probably have a mustache and long hair and everything. I probably wouldn't know one if I saw one." (23)

The subject of the Black 14 is still a very emotional one for Phil White four decades after covering the story for *The Branding Iron*.

"What still bothers me today is something nobody in authority wanted to face: the coach dismissed them from the team for wearing black arm bands on their civilian clothes the day before the game. By doing so they had violated his rule that scholarship athletes could not participate in demonstrations. The coach's action was a blatant and unquestionable violation of their right to free speech," White said. "The first thing the leaders and the lawyers involved should have done was to overrule that decision by the coach and put them back on the team. There were four lawyers on the board, including the governor, and if they had immediately stood up for the Bill of Rights, a compromise could have been worked out and this would not have become the tragedy it did." (9)

The vast majority of the 14 turned out to be just fine, personally and professionally, after being kicked off the Wyoming football team.

Within a week of the dismissal, UW announced that the players could return to the team the next season and that their scholarships would be continued through graduation whether they returned to the team or not. As a result, Griffin, Hamilton, Joe Williams and Meadows earned degrees in education.

Willie Hysaw, now known as Guillermo Hysaw, went on to receive a bachelor's degree in psychology at Oakland University, advanced MBAs in strategic management and financing and a master's degree in marketing from Claremont Graduate School before a distinguished career in the automotive industry that included being a vice president at Toyota Motor Sales USA, Inc., and a partner of Mach-I Autogroup LLC.

Lionel Grimes played baseball at Findlay University before starting his own successful career in the auto business; he is semi-retired and living in Columbus, Ohio.

"I talk about it when it comes up. A lot of young guys I talk to now don't even remember John Carlos in the Olympics," Grimes said. "I don't dwell on it. It was a learning experience and I'm not bitter."

Despite missing most of his senior season in 1969, Joe Williams played in the NFL for the Dallas Cowboys and New Orleans Saints; he lives in Richardson, Texas. Tony McGee transferred to Bishop College and then played 14 years in the NFL, winning a Super Bowl with the Washington Redskins; he still lives in the D.C. area and hosts a regional TV sports show.

Griffin returned to the Cowboys in 1970 and played for Eaton, along with Meadows and Ted Williams, and later joined Fritz Shurmur's staff at Wyoming before a successful career in the corporate world; he is semi-retired and living in Denver. Meadows went to work for Ford Motor Company after graduation and later went into the restaurant business; he is currently a realtor in Seattle.

Earl Lee is a retired principal and lives in the Baltimore area. He remains friends with Tony Gibson and his wife Barbara, who work and reside in their native Pittsfield, Massachusetts.

Hamilton has been a coach, teacher, principal and administrator in Casper, Wyoming, where he still lives. Ron Hill is also an educator in the Dallas / Fort Worth area.

"That list of names—there isn't one guy that was ego driven. Confident, yeah. Ego driven, no," Griffin said. "Just darn good athletes and good guys who went on to be pretty successful."

The group has lost track of Ivie Moore, who was incarcerated in Arkansas at one time, and Ted Williams, who was on track for a degree in engineering when he returned to play at UW in 1970. Jim Issac passed away in the early 1980s.

The Black 14 incident was perhaps harder on some than others, but the players involved can look you in the eye to this day and tell you that they walked into Eaton's office with the best of intentions.

"It kind of scared me at first because I knew every one of the Black 14 could have played pro. I knew if we stood up it could damage our careers," Moore said. "But I knew that at some point in time you've got to stand up for what you believe in.

"And after thinking about it, I stood up." (9)

The following photos courtesy of the UW Photo Service.

- First photo: Wyoming head coach Lloyd Eaton works the sideline at War Memorial Stadium.

- Second photo: Gene Huey makes a catch against Air Force at War Memorial Stadium.

- Third photo: Jim Kiick runs for a big gain against BYU.

- Fourth photo: Wyoming quarterback Paul Toscano looks for an opening.

- Fifth photo: Mel Hamilton (foreground) attends a Wyoming student protest before the UW-BYU basketball game wearing his Black 14 armband.

Coach Lloyd Eaton

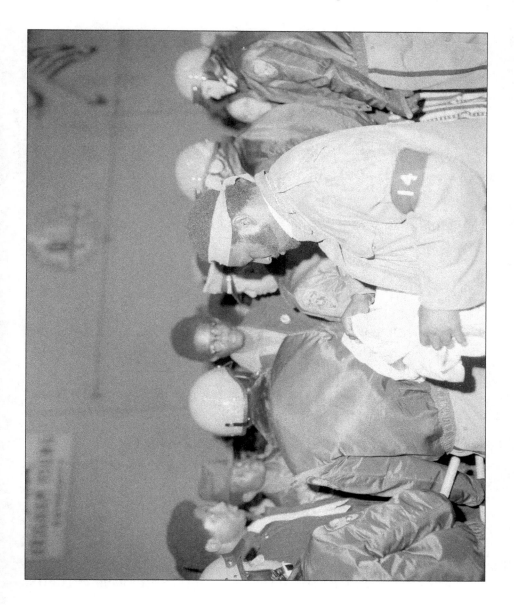

Sources

Interviews with Keith Burman, Dave Christensen, Tony Gibson, John Griffin, Lionel Grimes, Mel Hamilton, Tommy Hudspeth, Gene Huey, Earl Lee, Tony McGee, Don Meadows, Dave Montgomery, Larry "Bo" Nels, Paul Roach, Doris Shipley, Sally Ann Shurmur, Alan Simpson, Randy Welniak and Phil White were conducted during the winter and spring of 2009.

(1) Sugar Bowl Classic, A history, by Marty Mule, mainstream media international, 2008
(2) Longmont Times-Call, 'Live & Learn,' by Ryan Thorburn, Nov. 14, 1999
(3) Quote found at www.boystown.org
(4) Wilmington Race Riot Commission report found at www.history.ncdcr.gov/1898-wrrc
(5) Longmont Times-Call, 'Outside the lines,' by Ryan Thorburn, Nov. 14, 1999
(6) Laramie Boomerang, Oct. 22, 1969
(7) American Heritage Center archives, #10405, Box 1, Folder 8
(8) Laramie Boomerang, column by Larry Birleffi, Oct. 19, 1969
(9) University of Wyoming Television, "The Black 14" produced by Mike McElreath and Dr. Niyi Coker, copyright 1997
(10) American Heritage Center archives, #10405, Box 1, Folder 1
(11) UPI story printed in the Denver Post, Oct. 20, 1969
(12) Denver Post, Oct. 22, 1969

(13) Sports Illustrated, "No Defeats, Loads of Trouble," by Pat Putnam, Nov. 3, 1969

(14) 1. The State Press (Tempe, Arizona), "U of A Campus Simmers Weeks After Near Riot," Feb. 10, 1970. 2. Found in the Master's Thesis: Racism, Mormonism, and Black Protest, by Clifford A. Bullock, May 1992

(15) 1. Colorado State Collegian (Fort Collins, Colo.), "Protests, Bomb Mar CSC Match with BYU Athletes," Jan. 19, 1970. 2. Found in the Master's Thesis: Racism, Mormonism, and Black Protest, by Clifford A. Bullock, May 1992

(16) 1. Colorado State Collegian (Fort Collins, Colo.), "Halftime Protest Erupts; Seven Persons Arrested," Feb. 6, 1970. 2. Found in the Master's Thesis: Racism, Mormonism, and Black Protest, by Clifford A. Bullock, May 1992

(17) 1. The Daily Universe (Provo, Utah), "Mob Gathers as Marchers Walk Onto Floor," by Mike Twitty, Feb. 6, 1970. 2. Found in the Master's Thesis: Racism, Mormonism, and Black Protest, by Clifford A. Bullock, May 1992

(18) Casper Star-Tribune, "10 For the Ages," by Ron Gullberg, Nov. 1, 1997

(19) Research by Phil White with help from the University of Wyoming Sports Information Department

(20) Laramie Boomerang, 'Looking back: Curt Jimerson: a difference-maker,' by Bob Hammond February 19, 2005

(21) A Million Cheers: 100 Years of Wyoming Cowboy Football, by Steve Weakland, published by the UW Football Centennial Committee

(22) The New York Times, Frank Litsky's obit on Shurmur, Aug. 31, 1999

(23) Findlay.edu

(24) Denver Post, May 9, 1982

Biography

Ryan Thorburn is a sports writer for the Boulder Camera. Growing up in Casper, Wyoming, his heroes were always Cowboys—from Curt Gowdy to Fennis Dembo. Ryan attended the University of Wyoming and graduated with a degree in journalism before getting his first real break in the newspaper business at the *Casper Star-Tribune*. He was hired to cover the Denver Broncos beat for the Camera in 2000. Over the years he has broken some big stories (Patrick Roy's retirement from the Colorado Avalanche) and covered some big events (the Colorado Rockies' run to the World Series). This is Ryan's first book.

Books from Pearn and Associates, Inc.

Mathematics in Color,
Joseph J. Kozma

A Lenten Journey Toward Christian Maturity,
William E. Breslin

Walking in Snow,
John Knoepfle

I Look Around for my Life,
John Knoepfle

Ikaria: A Love Odyssey on a Greek Island,
Anita Sullivan

Goulash and Picking Pickles,
Louise Mae Hoffmann

Point Guard,
Victor Pearn

Books may be ordered through amazon.com, barnesandnoble.com, your local bookstore, (Ingram Books) you may order for libraries through (Baker and Taylor), and books may be ordered directly from the publisher at: <u>happypoet@hotmail.com</u>.